D1544527

MANAGING RISK
IN THE
SECONDARY
MARKET FOR
RESIDENTIAL MORTGAGES

Mortgage Bankers
Association of America
Washington, D.C.

Probus Publishing Company
Chicago, Illinois

© 1989   The Mortgage Bankers Association of America.

ALL RIGHTS RESERVED. No part of this publication may be reproduced, stored in a retrieval system, or transmitted by any means, electronic, mechanical, photocopying, recording or otherwise, without the prior written permission of the publisher and the copyright holder.

This publication is designed to present, as simply and accurately as possible, general information on risk management techniques and strategies in the secondary market for residential mortgages. It should be noted that the information presented is not all inclusive. Processes may have altered due to rapid changes in the industry. This publication should not be used as a substitute for referring to appropriate experts and is sold with the understanding that the publisher is not engaged in rendering legal, accounting, or other personalized professional service. If legal or other expert assistance is required, the services of a competent professional should be sought.

Library of Congress Cataloging-in-Publication Data Available

ISBN 1-55738-092-9

Printed in the United States of America.

1   2   3   4   5   6   7   8   9   0

Table of Contents

Table of Contents

Preface

Managing Risk in the Secondary Market for Residential Mortgages is the first book to be published by the Mortgage Bankers Association of America (MBA) on the critically important topic of managing the risk associated with originating and selling mortgage loans. The book is a product of considerable effort over several years by members of MBA's Risk Management Subcommittee and MBA staff of the Residential Finance/Government Agency Relations and Education Departments.

The development of this book would not have been possible without the time, expertise, and close cooperation of expert risk managers from the mortgage banking industry. Ralph D. Vermilio of Mortgage First Corporation, Atlanta, Georgia, was chairman of the Risk Management Subcommittee at the time this book was published, and much of the work was also accomplished under former chairpersons William R. Godfrey of All Valley Mortgage, Walnut Creek, California, and Jean Alperstein of A.S.K. Mortgage Corporation, Denver, Colorado.

MBA gratefully acknowledges the time and effort of the following contributing authors of this book: Jean Alperstein; William Coppedge, Nomura International Securities, Chicago, Illinois; William J. Denton, Sears Mortgage Corporation, Riverwood, Illinois;

William R. Godfrey; Rick W. Hollenberg, Security Financial & Mortgage Corporation, St. Louis, Missouri; George M. Olson, Dovenmuehle Mortgage Inc., Schaumburg, Illinois; Douglas H. Scheunemann, United Mortgage Corporation, Bloomington, Minnesota; J. Lee Summerlin, IBM Credit Corporation, Stamford, Connecticut; and Thomas G. Thompson, Chicago Board of Trade, Chicago, Illinois.

In addition, considerable assistance in critiquing and editing this book was provided by Deborah Allen-Malzahn, Mortgage Bankers Association of America; Jean Alperstein; Michelle V. Campbell, Mortgage Bankers Association of America; Don Coots, First Nationwide Bank, San Francisco, California; Steven Cox, B. F. Saul Mortgage Co., Chevy Chase, Maryland; Rick W. Hollenberg; Bill Lund, Citytrust, Inc., Bridgeport, Connecticut; Joseph B. McGougan, Amcore Mortgage Inc., Rockford, Illinois; John C. Radin, Weyerhaeuser Mortgage Company; Thomas G. Thompson; Barbara B. Waller, Peat Marwick Main & Company, New Orleans, Louisiana; and Ralph D. Vermilio.

Special appreciation is extended to George M. Olson, who coordinated the final technical review and edit of the book and to Ronald L. Rowland.

1

Defining Sources of Risk

Risk is the degree of possibility of loss. In mortgage banking, it is not possible to originate mortgages and eliminate 100 percent of the risk. The objective of the mortgage banking firm is to avoid, or at least minimize, potential losses due to risk exposure.

Internal Risk

The level of acceptable internal risk is controlled by the firm's senior management Once the level of acceptable risk has been decided upon, management monitors conditions affecting the firm's level of exposure and makes operating decisions based on corporate objectives and market conditions.

Corporate objectives license risk-taking. Senior management sets production and profit requirements as well as approves loan product, hedging vehicles, and broker-dealer relationships. All of the objectives may not be compatible over time because market conditions test the balance between volume requirements and profit margins, salability of new products, accuracy of reporting systems, adequacy of capital, commitment to objectives, availability of warehouse lines, and ability to adapt to marketplace dynamics. The ability to adjust to the many variables is the real life examination of a firm's business acumen.

Price

Loan pricing is the art of balancing the demands of production for a competitive advantage with the mandates of the firm's profit expectations. Pricing should minimize losses without compromising volume, and it is the first stage of the production cycle. Thus, pricing signals the firm's entrance into the arena of interest rate risk. By setting a price/rate, a firm actually accepts risk. The duration of that risk is defined by the term of the price guarantee.

Price guarantees on loans to borrowers are the greatest single source of risk in mortgage origination and the root cause of most marketing inefficiencies. They are unilateral agreements rarely enforced for the benefit of the issuer. The "free put" is an invitation to abuse; the borrower pays no fee, yet receives an enforceable agreement for performance at a specified yield. This applies to guarantees of any term: 5-10-30-60-75-90 days. Once a firm issues a guarantee, it accepts interest rate risk. The exposure to interest rate risk endures until the guarantee expires; but it is a risk that can be managed.

If a firm has gone long (more loans guaranteed to borrowers or funded than sold to investors) and interest rates rise, the guaranteed loans will sell for less than they were bought. If it is caught short (more commitments to investors than guaranteed loans to borrowers) during falling interest rates, it will pay more for the loans needed to fulfill commitments to investors. The risk in either case is defined as the difference between the price guaranteed to the homebuyer or investor and the market value of the loan. The higher the interest rate volatility and more time between commitment and sale of the loans, the greater the risk.

A second tier risk in setting price is the capacity of support staff to complete the production cycle on schedule. A firm's pricing policy assumes completion of processing, approval, closing, insuring/guaranteeing, and shipping functions within certain time parameters. Surges of volume, loss of staff, and agency approvals all affect the timing of delivery.

Price must consider delivery, not only as a calendar event, but also the type of delivery, (e.g., whole loan, security, participation). Securitized loan delivery can be cheaper than whole loan, but the latter offers the advantage of selling in individual units. Changes in delivery schedule or delivery vehicle pose price risk because the firm may be stuck with an inventory of loans it is unable to sell at a favorable price.

There must be a reasonable time correlation between pricing and delivery because the more time that elapses between application and delivery, the higher the risk and the greater the risk premium demanded by the capital market.

Pipeline

Pipeline is defined as the production cycle from application through closing; or application through cancellation. Within the pipeline there are guaranteed and float loans. The former are exposed to price risk if not matched with investor commitments. The latter pose no interest rate exposure until the loan is closed; the borrower retains the risk until closing, when the float loan leaves the pipeline to become part of inventory. If all loans floated to closing, marketing risks would be virtually non-existent. Similarly, if all guaranteed loans were certain to close, marketing risks would drop dramatically.

No loan is entirely certain to close. Any loan application that does not close is described as fallout; fallout can range from 10 to 50 percent of all loan registrations at the retail level, and upwards of 75 percent in wholesale and correspondent pipelines. Declining interest rates, low appraisals, buyer remorse, and bad credit, among other things, are all reasons for fallout. But no matter the cause, unexpectedly high fallout may mean problems in fulfilling investor commitments while unexpectedly low fallout may cause problems in finding enough commitments for guaranteed loans. Thus, fallout, coupled with price risk, is the pipeline's greatest risk.

Rising interest rates reduce fallout by increasing the incentive for a borrower with a guarantee to close at a then below market rate. Potentially significant losses can be sustained due to rapidly deteriorating market prices unless the pipeline is properly covered. Declining rates increase fallout due to borrowers transferring their loans to the cheapest price on the street. Refinance customers can worsen the problem as they continue to wait for the best price.

A fallout ratio is derived from historical averages of the percentage of unclosed loans. For a given production time period, (i.e. 180 days) fallout is computed as:

[Total Starting Pipeline $ + Total Applications $] – [Total Ending Pipeline $ + Total Closings $] = Total Fallout

Fallout Ratio

$$\frac{\text{Total Fallout (Dollars)}}{\text{Total Applications (Dollars)}} \quad = \quad \text{Fallout Ratio}$$

At times these calculations may prove inaccurate predictions due to sudden shifts in interest rates, pipeline product mix, shifts in the number of refinances, builder delays, or various other reasons. Marketing strategies are therefore subject to risk associated with changes in expected fallout.

Another pipeline risk is the reporting system. It is designed to alert the firm to the volume of loans guaranteed by product type and the duration of the guarantee periods. No marketing effort can defend against the risks of a deficient information system. The adage "garbage in, garbage out" is an especially apt description of faulty reporting. Whether the system is manual or fully automated, the database generated by the information system is central to any risk management plan, and its integrity must be a first priority. The pipeline is dynamic and in a state of constant transition. It is continually redefined by new applications, new loan types, expired guarantees, loan closings, and cancellations. Timely and accurate reporting is therefore essential.

Coverage

In addition to risks associated with pricing and fallout, there is the exposure that results from coverage, that is, covering (or choosing not to cover) loans with commitments in order to transfer interest rate risk.

The goal of marketing is to sell loan product to an investor and protect the potential marketing value created. That sale, whether optional or mandatory, is "shortening" risk:

Short = Sell

Conversely, a firm can choose not to sell and assemble an inventory of loans comprised of either pipeline, closed loans or both. By this strategy it lengthens its risk.

Long = Unsold

In daily operations, a firm can sell loans from the pipeline before they close for delivery at a time in the future—a "forward" sale commitment. If the company ends up selling more product than it actually closes, to make "good delivery" it pairs off by buying loans or securities from other lenders or dealers to fill forward sale commitments.

When loan prices in the secondary market are falling (interest rates are rising), more of the pipeline will close because borrowers do not want to forfeit their guarantee in the face of rising interest rates. A mortgage originator may be able to estimate origination volume and obtain coverage in anticipation of incoming applications.

At other times, when secondary market prices are rising (interest rates are falling), loans "in the money" (priced below current market price) may change a firm's perception of risk. The originator may be willing to accept more risk and goes "long." Should the market reverse, the risk is translated into price reduction at delivery.

Risk in coverage is the amount of sale and the timing of sale. A firm incurs interest rate risk if it sells too much (goes short), or if it sells too little (goes long). Change in rates punish or reward excess in either direction. Pipeline loans react to changes in interest rates, and hedges must be adjusted accordingly.

Investor Default

An investor backing out of whole loan commitments is a major risk that is especially strong in times of rising interest rates. Investor default may also be caused by the timing of delivery, a mismatch between investor specifications and the actual product, or lack of quality in the loans delivered. Any investor default will cause a firm to go long until a new investor is found. Because non-conforming loans are normally originated for a specific investor, should an investor renege, the firm may be faced with serious difficulties selling the loans. It is essential to analyze the financial capacity and verify the business reputation of an investor before signing a commitment.

Product

Product risk occurs in two forms. The first risk is that the loan product is not attractive to the public and loans cannot be originated. In that case a firm's losses are usually confined to research/development and promotional costs.

The second and possibly greater product risk is inability to sell the product to the secondary market. Fixed-rate, level-payment terms comprise a standard mortgage loan; the more exotic and complicated a new program, the narrower the field of investor. The adage "don't originate it if you can't sell it" finds root in product risk. The idea that non-standard products can always be sold at "some price" only disguises product risk as price risk; it does not change the risk.

In addition, non-standard products, by virtue of unique characteristics, frustrate established pricing models and systems, often making the transfer of interest rate risk difficult. Further, servicing systems may not be able to accommodate unique products and cost-effective servicing can become a problem.

At low interest rates, 30-year fixed-rate mortgages are the norm because a greater percentage of borrowers perceive them as the best value and most secure. But as rates rise, the number and variety of products increases to attract borrowers. The steepness of the yield curve has a major impact on originations. With spreads between one-year and 30-year yields at 250 basis points or more, originators promote adjustable rate mortgages (ARMs) in order to qualify buyers; for some buyers 15-year loans can be an attractive alternative to 30-year loans. When rates are high, builders will pay the maximum amount of points to qualify buyers for subsidized buydowns and deeply discounted note rates.

The broader the range of rates, the greater the marketing risk since it becomes more difficult to accumulate a poolable supply for each specific coupon. Market fluctuations can vary dramatically between premium and discount coupons; and the issue of whether to form GNMA II pools, Mini-macs, or multi-issuer FNMA pools will need to be addressed.

Product variations are not only difficult to manage, but origination and underwriting problems also generally rise as the number of loan programs and investors increase.

Extensive training must be coordinated for underwriters, shippers, originators, and closers to ensure that the proper documents are used, initial disclosures are completed properly, and all investor requirements are met. If these conditions can be met simply, risk can be decreased.

Delivery

Delivery is the end of the production cycle. It is presentation to the investor of the loan documents required prior to payment on purchase. Delivery requires coordination of the flow from pipeline through closing; coordination with the "back room" in shipping, insuring, and obtaining guarantees; and coordination with the investors to negotiate, in advance, exceptions to standard "good delivery."

Delivery risk is the inability to make "good delivery." Meeting the requirements of "good delivery" may not be possible for a variety of reasons.

Hybrid, non-conforming loan types and jumbo loans can be especially susceptible to delivery risk, so all requirements must be detailed in a delivery/pooling/servicing agreement. Size, type, and timing of the delivery as well as recourse in case of problems or errors must be described in detail.

Private investors usually specify whether they prefer delivery on a flow basis or in bulk. In order to make the most efficient use of delivery choices, a company must carefully scrutinize personnel requirements because inadequate staffing will result in late deliveries.

Delivery risk due to human error can be greatly reduced with computerization. A typographical error in a loan amount on a Ginnie Mae pool schedule, for example, can result in the lender reducing the principal balance to match what is typed, or possibly repurchasing the loan at par to place into another pool at the correct amount.

Another advantage of automation is that investors may allow an extended delivery period if a computer is used to transfer the information. For instance, when the schedule is completed manually for fixed rate Fannie Mae mortgage-backed securities pools, it must be received eight business days before delivery of the securities. But Fannie Mae allows receipt six days before delivery when a computer is used for transmission of schedules; the risk of human error is reduced and the marketing manager has two extra days for receipt of files. This may allow the loans to be sold at an later date, perhaps at a higher price.

There is still an inherent risk associated with input error into a computer; however, it can be greatly reduced through checks on maximum loan amounts, automatic calculation of P&I, and ensuring that the principal balance never exceeds the loan amount except in the case of a graduated payment mortgage loan.

Quality

Quality means conforming to requirements; quality risk is retribution for non-conformance; it is the cost of doing things wrong. All investor and agency agreements speak to performance standards and remedies for inferior quality. That language includes: recourse, no-bids, indemnification, repurchase, suspension, termination, and litigation. Poor quality loans are those that do not conform to regulatory, investor, and insurer/guarantor requirements related to disclosures, underwriting, appraisals, and documentation.

The concern with quality has become one of the most acute problems the mortgage industry faces today. At times the appreciation of real property has dramatically slowed and in some areas depreciation is the norm. Since the property's current value does not justify its debt, borrowers sometimes abandon the properties and the mortgage debts. In response, investors, agency insurers/guarantors, and private mortgage insurers have become more stringent and are invoking recourse actions as never before. This has had significant impact on quality risk. Lenders cannot hedge on quality and the costs of poor quality are substantial.

For example, FHA/VA foreclosures in some areas are averaging $2,500 loss per loan. Even worse is the VA's use of "no-bids," where the lender is forced to take title to a piece of foreclosed property when VA feels the loss will exceed their guaranty amount. These losses can be as much as $20,000 to $30,000 per property.

FHA/VA loans are typically sold through collateralization into Ginnie Mae pools, which require the advance of principal, interest and, Ginnie Mae escrows while delinquent. Here the lender incurs lost opportunity costs on the funds advanced.

In the conventional arena, Fannie Mae and Freddie Mac now require loans that default in the first four payments be repurchased. This places the burden on the lender for excess costs of foreclosure and liquidation above what the private mortgage insurer will pay.

Strict adherence to underwriting and appraisal requirements has become particularly important to avoiding onerous recourse actions imposed by insurers, guarantors, and investors when borrowers default. Mortgage insurance claims may be rejected and repurchase may be required by investors.

Quality sometimes trades at a premium. Investors may offer preferential pricing or special concessions if a company consistently delivers good, clean loans. (However, mortgage-backed securities trade on a generic basis and preferential pricing or concessions are not available.)

The marketing staff must have loan auditors to ensure compliance with requirements as well as complete and accurate documentation in the loan files. Adequate training sessions must be provided on an on-going basis for marketing personnel to keep up with all investor, insurer, and regulatory compliance changes. This will ensure delivery of quality loans in a timely manner.

External Risks

External risks are beyond a firm's control. They are market driven and reflect the market's adjustment to changing yield requirements.

Interest Rate Volatility

Interest rate volatility, the primary external risk, is the tendency toward consequential changes in yield. High volatility represents opportunity for speculators but jeopardy for risk-adverse hedgers. A firm's risk during periods of high volatility relates to its exposure; the more exposure, the greater the risk. When a firm encounters adverse price movement with significant exposure, its loans move "out-of-the-money"; they lose price value.

The firm's response to interest rate risk relates to coverage. Does it cover immediately and take its loss? If it does not cover, and price continues to deteriorate, its loss will swell. Volatility is generally characterized by choppy up and down patterns; sudden drops often are retraced by rallies as the market seeks a stable price level. Unless it uses disciplined approach, a firm risks following an explosive series of price adjustments and becomes a naive contributor to the speculators' windfall.

Even without exposure, interest rate volatility still poses a threat. Sudden reduction in rates accelerates fallout, while sudden increases in rates reduce fallout well below normal levels.

Basis Risk

To guard against changes in interest rates a firm will hedge. One hedging technique is the substitute sale. Instead of selling or buying loans, it sells and buys financial instruments. The substitute sale and the mortgage product are expected to have similar price reactions to changes in the marketplace. Basis risk occurs in a substitute sale when the value of a mortgage product and the value of the corresponding hedge vehicle do not respond to interest rate changes with identical dollar adjustments. A firm makes substitute sales because it believes basis risk is more manageable and less volatile than interest rate risk. There is no way to completely eliminate basis risk but it can be greatly reduced by proper management.

Consider the following situation, termed a "cross hedge." A company sells Treasury Note futures as a substitute sale against the Ginnie Mae pipeline—the T-Note is a Treasury security and Ginnie Mae is a mortgage-backed security. Because of the maturity and prepayment differences inherent in the instruments, changes in interest rates will produce similar (but not exact) changes to market yield adjustments, and thus variances in price change (see Chapters 3 and 4). The difference in price response is the basis risk.

2

Risk Management Tools

Risk management tools were developed to manage price risk. Managing price risk in mortgage banking means "hedging," or attempting to minimize losses due to adverse market conditions. Hedging is risk transfer. Unfortunately, the word "hedging" for too many mortgage bankers implies an activity that is shrouded in mystery and fraught with danger. While there is no doubt that working with some hedging devices can be complex and should therefore be left to technical experts, senior management and other non-technical management staff need to understand the basic concepts and strategy implications of using various hedging tools.

Seesaw movements in interest rates during the mid-1970s and 1980s spurred the growth of a diverse group of tools used to hedge against interest rate risk. These tools or instruments may be classified in general as either mandatory or optional commitments. Mandatory commitments are agreements in which the firm is obligated to perform; optional commitments give the firm the right, but not the obligation to perform.

Only by understanding how these various hedging tools work can a firm decide if, how, and when it should use them. A firm can realize a competitive edge if it is aware of the price protection possibilities that some of these tools present and is able to use them effectively to reduce or eliminate potential marketing losses. Of course, no hedge is fool-proof in combatting losses, each presents certain advantages and disadvantages.

Mandatory Commitments

Mandatory commitments are agreements obligating a lender to buy or sell a particular loan product at a specified interest rate, price, and date. Mortgage bankers commonly use two types of mandatory commitments to hedge pipelines—(1) cash forward sales and (2) purchases or sales in the futures market.

Cash Forward Sales

Cash forward sales are the easiest and most common form of interest rate protection. They can protect pipeline and inventory product at a known price. The lender must be assured that enough pipeline product will close to fill the commitment and have confidence that the investor intends to purchase the product, regardless of adverse changes in interest rates.

A firm can sell mortgages forward in the cash market through a wide variety of vehicles: whole loans, participations, mortgage-backed securities, bonds, or collateralized mortgage obligations. The instrument used depends on the profile of the business, including volume of originations, loan types, conforming or non-conforming product, investor outlets, servicing capabilities, accounting objectives and familiarity and experience with the various market techniques for selling mortgages.

Advantages of Forward Sales. In addition to their ease and relatively low cost, one of the major advantages of forward cash sales is that when loan type and rate are projected accurately, forward mortgage sales have been specifically designed to best fit the product originated by mortgage originators.

Disadvantages of Forward Sales. Delivery and liquidity risk are the two major drawbacks of forward sales. Delivery risk sprouts from the seller's commitment to provide loans by a certain date, although for a variety of reasons such as miscalculation of loan fallout, delivery may not be possible. In case of failed delivery, the firm must buy back the position (pair-off) on the transaction.

Liquidity risk can increase the risk of non-delivery. Liquidity risk results from selling forward a scarce coupon or unique product that lacks an active two-sided market (a buy and sell offer) or requires a longer accumulation period before pooling. If enough product can not be originated to meet the commitment delivery date, the firm may be unable to purchase similar product from other originators to offset shortfalls in the pipeline. For this reason, the firm must determine how much of the product is issued, outstanding, and how actively it is traded, before committing to a sale.

A disadvantage of a well-executed forward sale is that it forecloses the opportunity for windfall gains in an improving market.

Futures

The futures markets provide an organized exchange through which the owner of a commodity, or financial instrument, can transfer the price risk associated with the product to another party: a speculator. This practice began in the mid-1800s to help farmers cope with exposure to fluctuation in commodity prices. But it was not until 1975 that futures trading evolved in interest-rate-sensitive debt instruments to aid institutions manage their risk. Money is a commodity, which reacts to demand through interest rates.

Basic Principles. A financial futures contract is a mandatory agreement to either make or take delivery, at a specified time in the future, of a given quantity of a financial debt instrument, at a price agreed upon when the contract is executed. Participants in the futures market assume a position, either by selling (going short) or buying (going long) a futures contract, by paying a small deposit that acts as a performance bond.

Specifically, a firm may sell futures contracts to protect the pipeline or closed mortgages that are not covered by commitments. Instead of selling product forward through a mandatory sale, a lender sells a corresponding number of futures contracts. Because futures are used only as a substitute sale for cash market transactions, the participants in the futures market do not intend to ship or receive the underlying debt instruments. When the firm decides to sell the mortgages, the lender purchases an identical number of futures contracts to offset the ones that were sold, thus liquidating its futures position, while simultaneously executing a mandatory forward sale.

If futures market prices fall, the lender can purchase the offsetting futures contracts at a lower price than it sold the original contracts. This gain should offset the lower value of the mortgages. Should prices rise, the reverse should happen, profits in the cash market offset losses in the futures market.

Through a long hedge, a firm can protect profits on mortgages covered by mandatory commitments yet to be filled. Instead of buying debt instruments in the cash market, it buys futures contracts. If prices rise, the firm profits from selling futures contracts for more than they originally cost. This gain should offset losses incurred in buying whole loans from other sources to replace loans that do not close. The opposite is true if prices fall: losses in the futures market should be offset with gains from selling mortgages at the commitment price, which will be higher than the current market price.

Basis Risk. Hedging with futures contracts will seldom lead to perfect coverage because of inherent differences between the cash and futures markets.

As basis risk is identified, remedial action needs to be taken or gains in the futures market will not equal or approximate losses in the cash market and vice versa.

A cross-hedge is created when a futures position with an underlying instrument other than mortgages is used to hedge mortgages. Cross-hedging increases basis risk because inherent differences between the mortgages and the futures instrument cause the two to respond differently to changes in interest rates.

Mortgage bankers always use a cross-hedge when trading futures. Usually, they buy and sell futures contracts on either of two long-term debt instruments: U.S. Treasury Notes and U.S. Treasury Bonds. Both are traded on the Chicago Board of Trade. With a combined average daily trading volume of $35 to $45 billion, T-Notes and T-Bonds are extremely liquid and are bellwethers of long-term interest rates.

In hedging with Treasuries, firms not only accept basis risk caused by using different markets (cash and futures), but also basis risk caused by using different instruments (mortgages and Treasuries). Thus, when hedging in the futures market, firms must realize in advance that mortgage and futures prices do not usually move up or down in exactly parallel patterns. The use of futures will then mean substituting basis risk for interest rate risk.

Basis risk does not preclude hedging with futures; it just makes the process more difficult. It also leaves opportunities for arbitrage. Arbitrage opportunities exist because the generally repetitive patterns of the basis movement (difference between cash and futures price) make it more predictable, and therefore less risky, than the singular movement of either the cash prices or the futures prices. However, basis risk does mean that a futures position should never be put on and left unwatched until it expires; it must be monitored constantly and altered whenever appropriate to reflect changes in the relative values of the cash and futures markets.

The Instrument Behind the Contracts. Exhibits 2.1 and 2.2 provide pertinent details about Treasury Bond and Treasury Note futures contracts, which are the primary instruments used by mortgage bankers to hedge their pipeline and inventories in the futures market. Briefly, a Treasury Bond or Treasury Note futures contract is a mandatory commitment to make or take delivery of deliverable grade U.S. Treasury Bonds or Notes at a specified time.

Margin Costs. A T-Bond or T-Note futures position is bought or sold with a small deposit, or margin (initial margin typically about $2,500 per contract) that guarantees financial performance. Each party either adds to, or receives money from, its margin account each trading day as the value of the contract changes (maintenance margin).

Exhibit 2.1
Highlights of United States Treasury Bond
Futures Contract

Basic Trading Unit:	U.S. Treasury Bonds with $100,000 face value
Price Quotation:	Percentage of par, e.g. 94–01 or 94 1/32 of 100 of a hypothetical 8% standard coupon; maturity of at least 15 years
Minimum Fluctuation:	1/32 of a point (1%) or $31.25 per contract
Daily Price Limit:	96/32 ($3,000 per contract) above or below the previous day's settlement price
Delivery Months	March, June, September or December
Last Delivery Date	Last business day of the month

Exhibit 2.2
Highlights of United States Treasury Note
Futures Contract

Basic Trading Unit:	U.S. Treasury Notes with $100,000 face value
Price Quotation:	Percentage of par, e.g. 94–01 or 94 1/32 of 100 of a hypothetical 8% standard coupon; maturity of 6 1/2–10 years.
Minimum Fluctuation:	1/32 of a point (1%) or $31.25 per contract
Daily Price Limit:	96/32 ($3,000 per contract) above or below the previous day's settlement price
Delivery Months	March, June, September or December
Last Delivery Date	Last business day of the month

The Futures Market Exchange. Futures contracts are traded only on organized exchanges, and all transactions are non-transferable and legally binding. Trading is regulated by the exchanges and overseen by the Commodities Futures Trading Commission, a government agency To ensure performance, all parties executing trades are represented by, and have all trades settled through, a Clearing Corporation. The Clearing Corporation stands between the individuals, firms, or dealers and the other side of the trade. In effect, all trades are with clearing houses so that the credit of the individual traders is not an issue in the transactions. In the event a trader cannot perform, the clearing house does, thus protecting the confidence and integrity of the Exchange.

As mentioned earlier, participants in the futures market do not intend to ship or receive the underlying debt instrument. To avoid making or taking delivery, traders lift their position prior to the delivery date by simply executing an opposite transaction for the same number of futures contracts; the underlying instruments never change hands. Again, the Clearing Corporation balances and cancels these open positions for its customers.

Speculators, unlike hedgers, take part in the futures market without offsetting positions in the cash markets. They try to profit by taking risks. They assume leveraged positions hoping that futures prices will move in a specific direction and produce large profits. Thanks to speculators who are willing to assume price risk, the futures market in certain instruments is very liquid and very efficient. Buyers and seller can trade volumes of contracts with only small price spreads.

Hedge Ratios. Unfortunately, the change in value of $1 million in futures contracts does not usually equal the change in value of $1 million in mortgages because of differences in yields and other characteristics which distinguish the futures and cash market instruments. In order to obtain as complete coverage as possible, a hedge ratio is needed which equates the face value and yield of the cash position to that of the futures contract.

For instance, if the hedge ratio of T-Note futures to GNMA 9s is one-to-two, or 50 percent, then $1,000,000 of the loan inventory is hedged by selling $500,000 of futures contracts. The ratio must also take into account the effect of changing interest rates on futures and cash yields.

There are several ways to calculate hedge ratios. Some involve regression analysis between the two instruments, while others value the duration, or the estimated actual life of the instruments by analyzing their cash flows over time. (Tables of conversion factors used to adjust futures prices for actual bond and note deliveries are used for deriving hedge ratios and will help identify the futures contract with the lowest net financing charges. These tables can be obtained from the Chicago Board of Trade Marketing Department, futures brokers, and dealers.)

Calculating Basis Risk. Hedge ratios should consider the effect of changing interest rates on the cash and futures contracts. This is done by tracking and measuring the basis; that is, the difference between the market price of the mortgages (cash price) being hedged and the market price of the hedge instrument (futures price). The fluctuations in this relationship create basis risk because they alter the number of futures contracts needed to protect the mortgages. For this reason, the basis must be watched closely over the life of the hedge.

The following formula is the basis calculation:

Cash Price – Futures Price. (98:16 represents 98 16/32, this format will be used throughout the text.)

Day 1 (98:16 – 92:16) = 6:00
Day 2 (98:00 – 91:16) = 6:16
                     16 = change in basis

The hedge ratio in this case is 50 percent, thus the change in the position basis is actually zero because the cash position changed by 16/32 and the futures position value changed by the same amount ($1.00 \times 50\% = 16/32$).

By marking the cash position and the futures position to market every day, the firm can determine if the hedge ratios being used maintain a position value of close to breakeven. For example:

Cash   day 1 – $1,000,000 inventory @ 98:16   = $985,000
            day 2 – market price   @ 98:00   = $980,000
                                                 =   (5,000)

Futures   day 1 – $500,000 T-notes   @ 92:16 = $462,500
              day 2 – market price   @ 91:16 = $457,500
                  + 5,000

Net Position Value = -0-

The Effects of Changes in Basis. Widening Basis in a Short Hedge. The results of a basis change depend on the relationship between the cash and futures prices when the hedge is initially placed. Assume that a firm is selling T-Bond futures to cover the pipeline. If the futures price is higher than the cash price when the hedge is initially placed and the basis widens, the mortgage banker will post rising losses. If rates fall, the loss on the hedge will outweigh the increased value of the pipeline, and if rates rise the loss on the pipeline will outweigh the gain in the futures market.

The following scenario illustrates this case for both rising and falling prices as the basis widens:

A firm is hedging $1,250,000 in pipeline loans with T-Note futures. Hedge ratio is 80 percent, so the firm agrees to sell (short) 10 T-Note futures contracts (face value $1,000,000).

	Day One	*Day 30*		*Day 45*	
		Price Rises	*Price Falls*	*Price Rises*	*Price Falls*
Cash Price	98:00	98:08	97:24	98:20	97:04
$ Gain/Loss =	0	$3,125	($3,125)	$7,812	($10,937)
Futures Price	102:00	102:12	101:28	103:08	101:24
$ Gain/Loss =	0	($3,750)	$1,250	($12,500)	$2,500
Basis	4.00	4:04		4:20	

If the cash price is greater than the futures when the hedge is placed, a widening basis means there is an advantage to hedging in the futures market. Consider the following example showing a futures price lower than that of the cash.

Narrowing Basis in a Short Hedge. The effect of a narrowing basis when shortening (selling) futures depends again on the relationship between the cash and futures price. If the futures price is initially higher than the cash price, a narrowing basis leads to positive results. But if the cash price is higher, it means negative results.

Exhibit 2.3 shows the effects of a widening and narrowing basis when cash price is greater than futures and vice versa.

Basis Movement in a Long Hedge. The ground rules above also apply to the purchase of futures contracts to protect the pipeline. If a firm were buying futures contracts (going long) to cover unfilled commitments, it would experience the opposite result. That is, if the cash price were initially greater than the futures, a narrowing basis would lead to gains, but it would cause losses if the reverse were true.

Opposite Movements in Yields. In extreme cases, pipeline yields and hedge market rates both move in opposite directions rather than by unequal amounts in the same direction. If both moves were adverse, the net loss would include the full loss of pipeline value *plus* the loss on the hedge position.

Basis Basics. The previous discussion should make it evident that an effective hedge using futures is impossible without the careful tracking of basis. In view of the impact of basis risk, an understanding of its composition is crucial. The following components of basis may change unexpectedly: sector spread, yield curve, relative supply.

Sector spread means that as interest rates fall, a short Treasury hedge may need to be reduced, because mortgage prices tend to rise less than those of the Treasuries. If interest rates climb, an addition to the same Treasury hedge would normally be required because the rate of change in mortgage prices typically moves more in line with changes in the value of Treasuries.

Another related source of basis movement is the yield curve. Lenders sometimes hedge 30-year mortgages with Treasury-Bond futures, but if a 12-year mortgage prepayment is usually assumed, the price of the mortgage will perform closer to that of a Treasury instrument with a far shorter maturity. A one basis point change in yield causes a significantly greater price movement on a 30-year bond than on a 10-year instrument; and 30-year mortgages because of amortization and prepayment, often trade closer to a 10-year note.

The relative supply of Treasury or mortgage securities is also important. As market yields fall, for example, an absence of scheduled Treasury offerings can cause rates to drop. At the same time, lower rates can encourage more mortgage originations,

Exhibit 2.3 The Effects of Shifts in Basis When Selling Futures

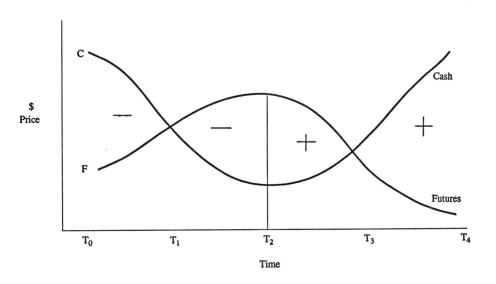

+ = Positive Change in Basis
− = Negative Change in Basis

$T_0 - T_1$ Negative Change: Cash Price Is Greater than Futures Price and Basis Is Narrowing

$T_1 - T_2$ Negative Change: Futures Price Is Greater than Cash Price and Basis Is Widening

$T_2 - T_3$ Positive Change: Futures Price Is Greater than Cash and Basis is Narrowing

$T_3 - T_4$ Positive Change: Cash Price Is Greater than Futures Price and Basis Is Widening

leading to more supply but not increasing demand among investors. In this case, mortgage rates fall correspondingly slower than Treasuries.

In some market contexts, liquidity is a major issue and the Treasury-to-mortgage spread widens as participants move to Treasuries from other fixed-income instruments. This shows that "basis drift" can occur independent of changes in interest rates—an important factor to consider when hedging with futures.

Basis risk may increase drastically if the hedge vehicle displays higher volatility than the mortgages it is purchased to protect. Volatility is a measure of how much an instrument's price fluctuates during a given period of time. If a highly volatile market causes a change in basis, the hedge ratio must be frequently adjusted by either selling or buying more futures contracts.

Advantages of Futures. Futures are more flexible than forward sales in protecting the value of uncommitted loans. The bid/ask spread tends to be less expensive for futures than the cash market. The liquidity of Treasury Notes and Bonds allows a futures position to be easily and quickly altered to reflect current market conditions; futures can be sold in amounts of $100,000 while many securities require minimum sales of $1 million; and because delivery is not contemplated in these contracts, product and delivery risk are minimized. However, in terms of transaction costs, hedge maintenance can be expensive.

Disadvantages of Futures. Using futures can be more costly and riskier than relying on forward sales. The existence of basis risk requires that futures contracts be actively managed by a trader who gauges movements in basis, volatilities, and anticipated changes in the market. There are cash flow costs to consider; a company can end up paying margin daily if futures move against the position.

Futures hedging is very vulnerable to dips or peaks in fallout because changes in the pipeline or cash position that hedge it have an immediate and direct impact on the cost effectiveness and relevance of the hedge. For these reasons, firms generally use the futures market only while accumulating the necessary applications (net of projected fallout) of a specific coupon or product to make a forward sale.

Optional Commitments

Lenders can protect against loan fallout and changing prices through optional coverage. This type of hedge gives the buyer the right, but not the obligation, to perform under the terms of the contract. Both optional and mandatory commitments specify rate, price (called the *strike* or *exercise* price), and length of contract; however, optional commitments also require an up-front fee (the "option premium"), paid to the writer for assuming the risk of potential delivery or purchase. Options are available in various combinations of mortgage yields, expiration months, and fees. The closer the yield on the option is to being "in-the-money," or the longer the term of the commitment, the higher the up-front fee.

Buying a put option to sell mortgages offsets the "free put" to borrowers and results in unlimited profits should prices rise, but it limits losses if they fall. The fee paid for the option represents the maximum potential cost to the holder regardless of the market price of the mortgage loans. If the market price improves and is greater than the strike price of the option, the lender will forego the option and sell into the immediate market.

In order to post a net gain on the transaction, the market price must change by at least the amount of the fee paid. It may be possible for the lender to recapture some up-front fees by reselling his option if it no longer has value in hedging his mortgages.

It is important to realize that the seller of the option takes an unknown risk in return for fee income. The option seller assumes the buyer will not deliver product if interest rates fall, and assumes the buyer will exercise the option if interest rates climb.

Types of Options

There are two types of option contracts: "calls" and "puts." A call option is the right to buy a security at a specified price: the exercise or strike price. Calls become more valuable as the underlying security price increases. A put option is the right to sell a security at a specified price; as the price of the underlying security decreases, the value of a put increases. Each type of option has a buyer (holder) and a seller (writer). (Although puts and calls are generally traded on the same underlying securities, it should be clearly understood that call options and put options are distinct investment vehicles—the buying and selling of a call in no way involves a put, and vice versa.) There are four possible positions in option trading:

Buy a Put:
Purchasing a put provides protection against a price decline below a strike price in exchange for the option premium (See Exhibit 2.4). Firms buy puts to protect their pipelines. The horizontal axis in Figure A represents the price of GNMA 9.5s at the option's expiration date. The vertical axis shows the profit or loss on the position. At any price level above 97 (the strike price), the option expires worthless, resulting in a one point loss because the premium paid for the option was one point. At a price of 96, the option allows its holder to sell securities one point above the then current market. At this price, the holder breaks even after paying the one point option fee. At a price of 94, the option generates to a two point gain.

Buy a Call:
Purchasing a call provides protection from a price increase above the strike price in exchange for the option premium (Figure B). Firms buy calls to cover unfulfilled commitments. At any price below 97, the holder loses one point. At 98, the call option buyer will break even after netting out the one point up-front fee. At any price above 98, the call option is profitable.

Sell a Put:
Writing (selling) a put provides the writer with fee income but exposes him to losses, potentially unlimited, should the market fall below the strike price (Figure C).

Sell a Call:
Writing a call also has limited applications for mortgage bankers. Although it provides the writer with fee income, it exposes him to losses, potentially unlimited, should the market rally above the strike price (Figure D). If prices are not expected to rise, however, call writing may increase fee in-

Exhibit 2.4

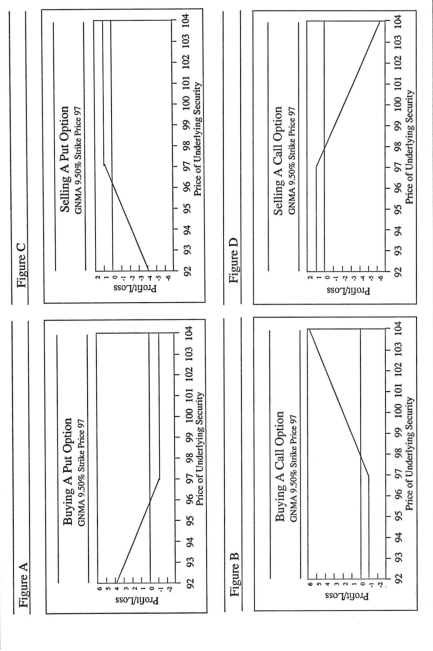

Figure A

Buying A Put Option
GNMA 9.50% Strike Price 97

Profit/Loss · Price of Underlying Security

Figure C

Selling A Put Option
GNMA 9.50% Strike Price 97

Profit/Loss · Price of Underlying Security

Figure B

Buying A Call Option
GNMA 9.50% Strike Price 97

Profit/Loss · Price of Underlying Security

Figure D

Selling A Call Option
GNMA 9.50% Strike Price 97

Profit/Loss · Price of Underlying Security

come, thus improving marketing results. Should the market remain stable, the mortgages may be sold outright and the call premium retained.

Margin Costs. Sellers, but not purchasers, of calls or puts must deposit margin with their broker to ensure delivery in case the option is exercised. If the underlying security is owned, it may be used as collateral; if not, a "naked" or uncovered position is assumed and margin payments are required. Margin requirements vary according to the different markets for options. Because of potentially hefty margins and unlimited losses, naked call writing is especially risky.

Interpreting Option Prices. The value of options is reflected in their premiums, and that value depends mostly on the difference between the strike price and that of the underlying security. The option premium has two components: intrinsic value and time value.

Intrinsic Value. The intrinsic value of an option is its worth if exercised immediately. It equals the amount by which the price of the underlying instrument is above the strike in the case of a call, or the amount by which it is below the strike price in the case of a put (See Exhibit 2.5). An in-the-money option is one that has intrinsic value. An option with no intrinsic value is out-of-the-money. Hence, a call option struck at 97 is in-the-money when the security is trading at 100, and out-of-the-money at 94. If the market for the underlying security is trading exactly at strike price, the option is at-the-money.[1]

Consequently, in-the-money options have higher premiums than those that are out-of-the-money because they have intrinsic value. If an option purchase is considered as a type of price insurance, then out-of-the-money options may be said to have a higher deductible; they hold more value for the owner than an option closer-to-the-money unless the market moves more than the difference in their premiums.

---

1   Woodward C. Hoffman, William J. Gartland, Nicholas Letica, *Hedging a Mortgage Pipeline*, Drexel Burnham Lambert, New York, NY (July 28, 1986): 4.

Exhibit 2.5

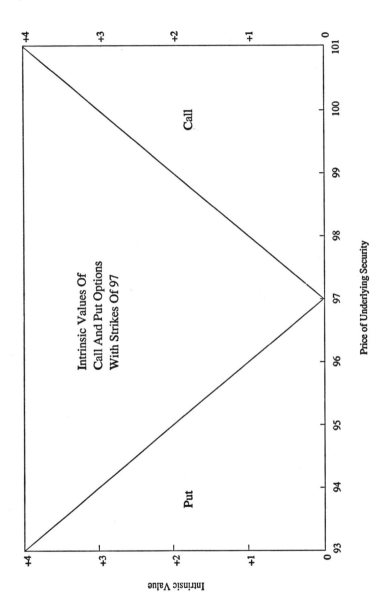

Intrinsic Values Of
Call And Put Options
With Strikes Of 97

Time Value. Prior to expiration, all options have some theoretical value above their intrinsic worth. One pays a fee for the option because there is always a chance, however small, that the market will move below the strike price for puts or above the strike price for calls.[2] Because this value declines as the option nears expiration, it is called "time value" and is the amount by which the premium exceeds the intrinsic worth. Consider the following put option example:

Put Option

FNMA 9.5 Price	94:00
Strike Price	96:00
Intrinsic Value	2:00
Time Value	1:16
Premium (fee paid)	3:16

Each 1/32 is worth $31.25, so 3:16 premium translates into $3,500 for each put option on a $100,000 FNMA 9.5 contract. Out-of-the-money options have a time value only, which is impacted by supply and demand, market volatility of the underlying security, and time to expiration.

Determining Option Premiums. Models, such as Black Scholes, have been developed to calculate the value of an option premium. A mortgage lender might use one of these models to select the put option with the highest strike price (lowest strike price in case of a call option and lowest premium in relation to the marketplace for various types of underlying debt instruments). These models consider several factors in determining premiums.

Market Price and Strike Price. The greater the market price in relation to the strike price, the greater will be the value of a call. If a call option is in-the-money, then the greater the market price of the underlying security, the greater the intrinsic value. For an out-of-the-money call option, the less out-of-the-money it is, the greater the probability that the call will trade into-the-money. For

---

2   Ibid., 4–5.

a put, the lower the market price in relation to the strike price, the higher the option premium.[3]

Volatility. The greater the price volatility of an option's underlying security, the greater the option's value. This is because greater volatility widens the likely trading range of the underlying market, increasing the likelihood that the option will trade into (or further into) the money. While there is also the likelihood of the option trading out-of-the-money, only the holder has the right to exercise. Therefore, the in-the-money situation carries more weight.[4]

Time to Expiration. Time to expiration is also positively correlated with an option's premium for much the same reason as volatility. A longer-term option with the same underlying volatility has a greater probability of trading into-the-money. The option's value is roughly proportional to the square root of the time of expiration. For example, if the time to expiration is doubled, then the value of the option will increase by approximately 141 percent (square root of two).[5]

Short Term Interest Rates. At any given forward market price, higher interest rates lower an option's premium to compensate for the premium's opportunity cost.[6]

Option Price Changes. Delta describes the rate of change in the value of an option as a percentage of the change in the underlying instrument. A put option with a delta of 65 percent, for instance, should increase in value by 65 basis points in price when the underlying instrument declines in price by one hundred basis points. The size of delta is affected by the amount of time remaining until expiration and by how much the strike price is in- or out-of-the-money. A deeply in-the-money option will have a delta close to one, while a deeply out-of-the-money option will have a delta close to zero. The change in the option's value can never be more than that of the underlying security, so delta is never greater than one.

---

3   Ibid, 5.
4   Ibid., 5-6.
5   Ibid., 6.
6   Ibid., 6.

In using options, the hedger must consider the trade-off between price and protection.

The Markets for Options

Firms may acquire options in three different forms: (1) standby commitments; (2) over-the-counter options on mortgages and mortgage-backed securities; and (3) options on futures contracts.

Standby Commitments. Firms can purchase standby or optional commitments to deliver loans to institutional investors for up-front fees ranging from one-half to two points. Typical of this kind of commitment are ones offered by Freddie Mac and Fannie Mae to their respective approved sellers, plus some thrifts, life companies, and pension funds.

Generally, a standby commitment will permit a firm at its option, to sell mortgages to an institutional investor at a specified price. Most standby commitments are puts.

Both Fannie Mae and Freddie Mac have standby or optional commitment programs that feature standard terms and product types. But the market in standbys is one-sided and not very liquid; that is, firms can only buy and sell standby commitments that are puts. (In addition, a firm who decides to sell rather than exercise a Fannie Mae or Freddie Mac standby commitment can only sell it to another approved seller, and it should be noted that the Fannie Mae standby, unlike the Freddie Mac optional commitment, must be converted to a mandatory commitment 30 days prior to delivery.)

Over-the-Counter Options. Over-the-counter (O-T-C) options may be bought on mortgage pass-through securities from various securities dealers who make a market in them. (The premiums are quoted in 32nds.) These options offer much flexibility to a firm in designing a hedge when compared to the standby commitment previously described. Unlike the traditional standby commitment where a lender can only purchase or sell a put, in the O-T-C market a lender may be able to purchase and sell (write) calls as well as puts. Therefore, mortgage bankers can take any side of an options transaction in structuring a hedging strategy.

In addition, the firm can tailor a hedge specifically suited to the pipeline by specifying exact expiration dates and either strike price or premium. Because they are individually tailored by the dealers who make a market in them, O-T-C options on mortgage-backed securities can suffer from a wide spread in bid/offer prices.

Hedging with O-T-C Options. In order to properly hedge a pipeline using a put with O-T-C options, a mortgage banker must determine how many contracts on the underlying mortgages are required to cover his cash position and then divide this number by the options' delta (dollar change in the price of the option for every one point price change in underlying mortgage security). If an O-T-C out-of-the-money option on FNMA 9.5s had a delta of 35 percent and the mortgage banker were hedging $800,000 of FNMA 9.5s in the pipeline, he would divide 8 by .35 to determine that 23 options contracts are needed to hedge. (Many brokers have developed models that assist lenders in formulating hedge ratios for options that take into account the impact of changing interest rates on the value of the underlying security and the resulting change in the value of the option.)

Options on Treasury Futures. Options on U.S. Treasury Note and Bond futures are traded on the Chicago Board of Trade under highly standardized terms. Contracts are exercised into futures contracts, so sizes are $100,000, and premiums are quoted in 64ths, or $15.625 per 1/64. Strike, or exercise prices, are set at two point intervals for bond futures, and at one point for T-Notes.

If T-Bonds are trading at 86.00 (86 0/64), for example, strikes may be set at 80, 82, 84, 86, 88, 90, and 92. Expiration dates fall about the third Friday of the month, one month prior to the delivery month of the underlying futures contracts. Options on December 1987 T-Notes and T-Bonds, for instance, expired November 21, and the last trading day was the 20th.

Chicago Board of Trade margin costs for selling options equal the option premium plus the greater of either (1) the current futures margin minus one-half the amount, if any (the option is out-of-the-money), or (2) one-half of the futures margin.

Hedging with Options on Futures. As with futures and O-T-C options, in order to use options on futures effectively, the lender must calculate a hedge ratio. Similar to O-T-C options, the delta is used to compute the number of options contracts needed to hedge. The lender first calculates the number of futures contracts that would be required to hedge a position, and then divides this by delta. The result is the number of options contracts that are needed to be fully hedged. For example, if ten futures contracts are required to hedge the pipeline, and the delta for out-of-the-money put options is 35 percent, then 29 out-of-the-money put options on futures should be purchased.

Options on futures expose the lender to more basis risk than O-T-C options because a change in the basis of the cash and futures position may alter the options hedge ratio. To maintain the desired hedge ratio, it is essential that changes in the relationship between cash and futures prices, as well as between options and futures prices (the delta), be monitored closely.

Options on Futures versus Standbys. The basic difference between options on T-Note and T-Bond futures and standby commitments is that when the futures option is exercised, the holder merely assumes a position in the contract; when the option on a mortgage commitment is exercised, the physical debt instrument changes hands.

Options on futures contracts can be cheaper than standby commitments. They are less costly when exercised because the holder simply assumes a margin position in the futures market instead of selling the actual instrument. Losses on the options position are limited to the premium paid, and underlying T-Bond or T-Note contracts can be exchanged later through offsetting transactions.

Options on Futures versus O-T-C Options. It is difficult to compare options on futures with O-T-C options because of differences in the underlying securities, premiums, and the amount needed to create a hedge. But in general, options on futures have several advantages, including:

- Greater liquidity;

- Smaller spread between bid and ask prices;

- Smaller minimum trades; and

- More flexibility in adjusting or closing positions.

On the other hand, the following disadvantages can also be encountered:

- Predetermined strike prices or premiums and expirations dates;

- Usually, require greater hedge ratios because historically an excess of futures contracts over mortgages is needed to hedge a position; and

- Higher basis risk due to differences between mortgages and the futures contract on T-Bonds or T-Notes.

Options Combos. There are several types of combination positions that can be created with O-T-C options or options on futures. Because they are complicated to implement, all of the options combos require an expert knowledge of the options market and are by no means for the initiate or a company just starting to use options.

A "spread" involves being both the buyer and writer of the same type of option, put or call, on the same underlying security but with different strike prices and/or expiration dates. A "straddle" involves either purchasing or writing both a put and a call on the same underlying security, with the options having the same strike price and expiration date. Spreads and straddles are high risk strategies and not used often by mortgage bankers.

Creation of "synthetic" options positions, on the other hand, are quite popular among mortgage bankers. A synthetic put is created by selling mortgages forward and buying a call simultaneously, or waiting until the market has bottomed out to buy the call. If the market recovers, profits are posted when selling the call. But if the market continues to fall, the firm is protected by the put option and merely loses the option premium. A synthetic call allows the firm to lock-in a price floor and is created by originating mortgages and buying puts.

"Compound" and "split fee" options are also now available over-the-counter. They are basically options on options and are referred to as calls on puts (ca-puts) and calls on calls (ca-calls). They require the buyer to pay a fee for the right to buy an additional option (extension) at a later date at a given strike price. The combined fee for the compound option is always more than required for the single premium option with comparable terms.

Advantages of Hedging with Options. Options are the only financial instruments that allow a firm to hedge downside risks of the pipeline and inventory without sacrificing potential upside gains; thus they are fast becoming the preferred means of hedging. A put can be viewed as an insurance policy. If the market falls, it covers the pipeline as would a forward sale. However, it is more flexible insofar as it leaves some upside potential in a strong market in exchange for the higher cost of the option.

Options are therefore good hedging devices for covering builder commitments, minimizing interest rate risk on pipeline loans, and introducing new products. In general, options are most valuable to the mortgage banker hedging the pipeline in markets that tend to be increasingly volatile. The wide variety of options available also affords a firm great latitude to determine the degree of protection. As previously mentioned, a firm may opt to obtain more protection for its pipeline by buying in-the-money puts, or it may decide it needs less protection and buy out-of-the-money puts.

Disadvantage of Hedging with Options. The use of options demands payment of up-front fees. A firm must establish a plan to recover front-end costs by charging borrowers additional fees, increasing the points charged at closing, or using the optional coverage to protect a larger volume of loans.

Constant monitoring of the options position is also required. It is critical to track expiration dates, because the option writer has neither the motivation nor responsibility to notify the holder when it becomes profitable to exercise the option. For O-T-C options and options on futures, additional constant monitoring of the position is required to track changes in the options hedge ratio. This is especially true in the case of options on futures because changes in basis between the cash and futures position must be taken into account.

3

How to Quantify and Measure Risk

After identifying its sources of risk and the tools available to manage that risk, a firm must take the next step and measure the extent of its exposure before it can prevent changing interest rates from eroding its profit margins. Internal risk measurement requires that a company analyze information about its pipeline, warehouse, interest rates, and prices and always read the results with an eye toward correction or improvement.

Measuring Internal Risk

Measuring internal risk often requires a firm to impose self-constraints and limits in its evaluative methods. The purpose of measurement is to develop data that will minimize risks. When the risk exposure outweighs the economic values that can be produced, business sense dictates a change in method.

Price Exposure

To measure price exposure, a firm requires accurate data that serves as a basis for its hedging strategy. The information is as follows:

1. *Current position*: The extent of gains and losses that would be incurred if the firm had to meet loan guarantees and mandatory commitments at today's market prices.
2. *Net mandatory position*: The difference, whether long or short, between current market values of guaranteed loans and mandatory commitments.
3. *Net non-mandatory position*: The difference, whether long or short, between the current dollar volumes of the discounted pipeline (adjusted for fallout) and optional commitments.
4. *Pipeline fallout*.
5. *Potential exposure if interest rates rise*.
6. *Potential exposure if interest rates fall*.

Data Sources

To measure price exposure and hedge risks successfully, the marketing department needs timely and accurate information on loans-in-process, closed loans, and commitments in order to assess the firm's market position. The establishment of a reliable marketing information network is essential to the accurate evaluation of market position and the successful execution of trades by the marketing department.

Creating and maintaining a marketing database that generates reliable market position reports can be a complex task for several reasons. First, information input will be required from a number of departments that are not directly concerned with the marketing of loans. For example, the originating branch offices must provide information on their pipelines—new applications, loans-in-process, and loan cancellations—and on newly closed loans, and the department responsible for warehousing and shipping must provide information about the total warehouse inventory of loans. Since warehoused loans are at least temporarily serviced by the firm, the servicing department must notify marketing of warehoused loans in default or foreclosure because delinquent loans will not be marketable. Further, the marketing department itself must maintain accurate information on commitments, hedges, and completed trades. It is incumbent upon senior management to establish the discipline and coordination among departments necessary to develop and maintain the required data.

The requirement for information to be accurate, timely, and complete necessitates the development of reliable mechanisms for gathering and reporting data, in addition to strict procedures, controls, and checking protocols. The use of automated systems for collecting the data and the establishment of a common database will greatly enhance a firm's ability to maintain timely marketing information and are essential for the mortgage banker with a large volume of originations.

Manual systems are cumbersome and inefficient with respect to staff time and they severely limit the ability to gather and develop required information in time to make critical decisions. The time that it takes to get pipeline and closed loan information represents an additional risk in a volatile interest rate environment. A marketing manager cannot hedge loans if they are not aware that the loans exist—a situation which can occur simply because of the time it takes to gather and disseminate information.

Finally, although a well-developed computer system can help solve the timeliness issue and reduce potential errors, the information resident in its database will be reliable only if accurate and complete data is input at the source—"Garbage in, garbage out."

Quantifying Price Risk

With an accurate marketing database, reports can be generated to quantify and evaluate a firm's price exposure. While the reports are a static depiction of a firm's market position at a given point in time, they are the best gauge of risk in daily transactions and should be continuously updated with new information at least once or twice each day.

Mark-to-Market. The most important tool that senior management and the risk manager have available to measure the results of their risk management policies is the mark-to-market report. This report values the inventory that has been sold against the sale price of the loans, and the unsold inventory/pipeline against either the current market (if the loans are not hedged) or against the value of the hedge instrument.

The mark-to-market report details the firm's current position —i.e., today's net profit or loss position of the inventory/pipeline —and is therefore the key to limiting risk.

Firms that access this information on at least a daily basis are subject to considerably less risk than those that can only provide the information less frequently. Any company that uses futures or options on futures cannot prudently manage its risk without a daily mark-to-market.

The particular format of a mark-to-market report may vary according to a company's operations and preferences. Exhibits 3.1 and 3.2 illustrate a typical report presented in two parts. The current profit or loss on the allocated (sold) inventory is shown in the first part, and the current position of the unallocated (unsold) inventory/pipeline is contained in part two.

The allocated report is a matchout of specific commitments with the loans that have been selected by the marketing department to fill those commitments. It also takes into consideration any new fees that have been paid or received for commitments during the current period. The gain or loss related to each commitment is the difference between the commitment sale price and the weighted average acquisition price for each loan category. The total gain or loss will change as sold loans are shipped and funded and as unsold loans are matched with specific commitments.

Exhibit 3.1 Marketing Position Report: Allocated

Investor	Commitment #	Commitment Expiration	Type	Term	Yield	Unfunded Volume (000's)	Wtd Avg Price	Sale Price	Gain (Loss)
WHOLE LOAN SALES									
FNMA	950007	01/05/85	FNMA ARM	15	10.50	510	89.564	90.225	$3,371
	965301	01/15/85	FNMA ARM	30	10.50	679	89.225	90.450	8,318
	976813	01/31/85	FNMA ARM	30	10.75	210	90.125	93.175	6,405
First Federal	2550	01/12/85	CONV	15	12.75	125	96.625	98.478	2,316
American	K1205	01/10/85	FHA GPM	30	11.00	150	90.725	93.267	3,813
Union Life	3005M	01/22/85	FHA GPM	30	11.00	90	91.000	94.125	2,813
TOTAL GAIN (LOSS)						1,764			27,036
FNMA TRADES									
Merrill Lynch	06116	01/15/85	CONV	30	12.75	414	96.335	98.879	10,532
	06234	01/23/85	CONV	30	13.00	368	97.225	99.425	8,096
Goldman Sachs	G56011	01/04/85	FNMA ARM	30	10.50	250	89.475	90.775	3,250
TOTAL GAIN (LOSS)						1,032			21,878
GNMA TRADES									
Salomon	20001	01/09/85	FHA/VA	15	11.50	670	91.575	94.670	20,736
First Boston	9077	01/18/85	FHA/VA	30	11.75	534	93.375	96.000	14,018
TOTAL GAIN (LOSS)						1,204			34,754
COMMITMENT FEES									
A G Becker	67890	02/15/85	FHA/VA	30	11.75				(10,000)
FNMA	990175	02/20/85	FNMA ARM	15	11.75				(9,000)
TOTAL									(19,000)
FNMA	995701	03/20/85	FNMA ARM	30	10.00				(9,000)
Universal	00456	03/25/85	CONV	30	12.00				(3,000)
Brubaker	66751	03/12/85	CONV	30	11.75				2,000
TOTAL									(10,000)
GRAND TOTAL NET GAIN (LOSS)						4000			54,668

Exhibit 3.2
Marketing Position Report: Unallocated

Long

Status	Type	Term	Rate	Volume (thous.)	Wtd Avg Price	Current Market	Gain (Loss)
Closing in	FHA ARM	30	11.00	1700	94.225	97.750	$59,925
thirty to	FNMA ARM	15	11.25	2050	93.995	98 125	84,665
sixty days	FNMA ARM	30	11.50	570	94.890	98.500	20,577
	FHA GPM	30	11.75	890	95.230	96.580	12,013
	FHA GPM	30	12.00	1624	95.012	98.379	54,680
	FHA/VA	15	12.25	6045	95.223	98.684	209,201
	FHA/VA	30	12.50	5123	95.134	100.000	249,285
	CONV	15	12.75	250	94.525	101.324	16,997
	CONV	30	13.00	400	93.675	103.649	39,895
	TOTAL			18652			747,238
Closing in	FHA ARM	30	11.00	1200	94.340	97.750	40,920
thirty days	FNMA ARM	15	11.25	789	95.150	98.125	23,473
	FHA GPM	30	11.50	1450	91.525	92.788	18,319
	FHA GPM	15	11.75	3217	93.550	94.580	33,127
	FHA/VA	15	12.00	3468	94.125	96.379	78,169
	FHA/VA	30	12.25	2870	95.250	98.186	84,260
	FHA/VA	30	12.50	2555	96.500	100.000	89,425
	FHA/VA	30	12.75	1976	97.000	101.821	95,264
	CONV	30	13.00	530	96.775	103.649	36,431
	TOTAL			18055			499,389
Closed in	FHA ARM	30	10.50	1324	92.678	97.000	57,223
warehouse	FNMA ARM	30	10.75	978	93.125	97.375	41,565
	FHA/VA	30	11.50	1500	90.125	92.788	39,951
	FHA/VA	15	11.50	4107	91.525	92.788	51,888
	FHA/VA	15	11.75	6570	93.375	94.580	79,152
	FHA/VA	30	12.00	5540	94.275	96.379	116,563
	FHA/VA	30	12.25	4290	95.000	98.186	136,674
	FHA/VA	30	12.50	2300	95.995	100.000	92,115
	CONV	30	1300	830	97.000	103.649	55,185
	TOTAL			27439			670,316
GNMA	Feb. 85		12.00	2000	94.225	96.379	43,080
calls	Feb. 85		12.50	1000	95.550	100.000	44,500
	Mar. 85		12.50	3000	96.000	100.000	120,000
	TOTAL			6000			207,580
	Total Long			70146			2,124,523
	Net Gain/(Loss)						1,454,926

Exhibit 3.2 (Continued)

Short

Type	Del. Date	Rate	Volume	Commit. Price	Current Market	Gain (Loss)
GNMA Regular	Jan.	11.00	5000	88.775	89.231	($22,794)
Mandatory	Jan.	11.25	5000	89.734	91.005	(63,566)
Delivery	Jan.	11.25	4000	89.995	91.005	(40,413)
	Feb.	11.50	4000	92.550	92.788	(9,536)
	Feb.	11.25	3000	88.550	91.005	(73,660)
	Feb.	11.50	3000	91.725	92.788	(31,902)
	Feb.	12.00	3000	93.889	96.379	(74,701)
	Mar.	11.75	4000	93.000	94.580	(63,190)
	Total		31000			(379,762)
GNMA ARM	Jan.	10.00	1000	90.225	96.250	(60,250)
Mandatory	Feb.	10.00	1500	89.889	96.250	(95,415)
Delivery	Mar.	10.50	500	90.500	97.000	(32,500)
	Total		3000			(188,165)
GNMA GPM	Jan.	11.50	1500	90.225	92.788	(38,451)
Mandatory	Feb.	12.00	1500	94.775	96.379	(24,060)
Delivery						
	Total		3000			(62,511)
FNMA ARM	Jan.	10.00	1000	94.334	96.250	(19,160)
Mandatory	Feb.	10.50	1000	95.000	97.000	(20,000)
Delivery						
	Total		2000			(39,160)
	Total Soft		39000			(669,598)

The allocated report is a significant part of the analysis of current market position for several reasons. First, although the gains and losses for each commitment are based on existing sales agreements, the firm still retains a measure of risk because investor funds have not been received. Second, the report provides the marketing staff with a mechanism for keeping the status of unfilled or partially-filled allocated commitments to ensure that sales agreements are being met in a timely manner. Status tracking of allocated commitments facilitates the identification of discrepancies in shipping loans or receiving investor funds and allows the marketing department to address problems that could violate agreements or damage investor relations.

Commitment fees must be considered in the calculation of marketing gains and losses, and the inclusion in the allocated report of the fees paid in the current accounting period, irrespective of the commitments to which they relate, is one legitimate method of reflecting their impact.[1] Another method is to reflect commitment fees by netting them against the particular commitments to which they relate. (The latter method can be difficult and cumbersome.)

In an ongoing operation, commitment fees are a recurring expense, and the timing of payment or receipt of these fees can vary depending on the terms of the related commitments. "An investor, for example, may require that a commitment fee be paid at the time the commitment is purchased, when the loans are actually delivered, or even a portion at the time of purchase and the balance at delivery."[2] Furthermore, some commitments require multiple deliveries spaced over periods of months, requiring detailed allocation and tracking methods to match commitment fees with particular commitments. The inclusion of all current period commitment fees in the allocated report is therefore a straightforward and simpler representation of their impact, especially for the purpose of evaluating market position.

The second half of the mark-to-market report, the unallocated report (Exhibit 3.2), details primarily the current gain or loss related to unsold loans, taking into consideration mandatory commitments and certain options. The "long" side of the report shows relevant information and gain or loss calculations for all guaranteed pipeline loans, all unsold closed loans in warehouse, any mandatory calls or purchases, and any in-the-money optional calls. The "short" side contains similar data for all unfilled mandatory commitments, any mandatory puts, and in-the-money optional puts that are available to cover the long position. For each position, long and short, a gain or loss is computed for each entry, and the totals for each side are netted to derive a net current unallocated position.[3]

---

1   Mortgage Bankers Association of America, *Marketing Information and Position Reports* (1985): 24.
2   Ibid., 25.
3   Ibid., 19.

The organization of the report, i.e., valuing loans and commitments separately rather than attempting to match them, reflects a philosophy or practice of managing total risk exposure instead of the risk associated with individual groups of loans. A matchout report requires that the weighted average price of each loan group be compared with the price of an assigned commitment in order to derive a single column of gains and losses similar to what appears in the allocated report.

"However, a matchout in the unallocated report is less useful from an operational perspective because it ignores the impact of current market rates on the current position and fails to consider the many alternative allocation choices that may exist. There are often a number of different commitments to which a particular group of loans could ultimately be allocated."[4] When it becomes necessary to meet a specific investor commitment, the choice of loans selected for the commitment will depend on how that matchout fits in with the firm's optimal strategy for its entire market position at the time of allocation.

The allocated report, if updated frequently, can be a dynamic tool for capturing and monitoring the current position of unsold loans. For example, the report may reflect losses on the long side and gains on the short side if market rates have risen steadily over the course of several months. Rising interest rates will deflate the current market values of unsold, guaranteed loans, thereby narrowing any previous gains and widening losses. On the short side, rising rates will increase the current market values of mandatory commitments entered into prior to the movement of rates, resulting in gains or narrower losses for fixed-price commitments. Conversely, a declining interest rate market will increase gains on pipeline and warehouse loans, and narrow gains or increase losses relating to fixed-price commitments.[5]

Because of their detailed orientation, both the allocated and unallocated components of the mark-to-market report will be used primarily by the risk manager, rather than senior management. In addition, it is necessary to combine the results of the two components to derive a total net current position for both sold and

4   Ibid., 20.
5   Ibid., 20.

unsold loans. Therefore, a mark-to-market summary report (Exhibit 3.3), which is a snapshot of the current and the year-to-date positions, should be developed for the use of senior management.

Exhibit 3.3
Marketing Position Summary

Status	Long	Short	Gain (Loss)
Allocated			54,668
Unallocated	2,124,523	(669,598)	1,454,925
Current Position			1,509,593
Balance in Reserve for Losses			300,000
Prior Periods Gains (Losses)			6,243,950
Total Prior Position			6,543,950
Year-to-Date Position			8,053,543

Floating Loans. Since the Mark-to-Market Report illustrated above contains only guaranteed and sold loans, another report is necessary to identify loans that remain unguaranteed, and floating at market.[6] The floating at market report in Exhibit 3.4 summarizes all the floating loans in the pipeline; it may also be used to list optional calls or puts that are out-of-the-money, but within several points of current market prices.[7]

Since the firm is not at risk with respect to loans floating at market or the optional commitments, they have no impact on the gain or loss calculations of the *current* market position. They can however significantly affect a firm's analysis of risk for the future.[8]

For example, if a large percentage of the pipeline is floating at market and the marketing department's coverage includes an excess of mandatory commitments over guaranteed loans, a certain percentage of the floating pipeline may need to close for the firm

6   Ibid, 25.
7   Ibid, 25.
8   Ibid., 25.

Exhibit 3.4 Marketing Position Report: Floating at Market

	Long					Short					
Status	Type	Term	Volume (000's)	Status	Type	Delivery	Rate	Volume (000's)	Commit. Price	Current Market	Gain (Loss)
Closing in thirty to sixty days	FNMA ARM	30	450	FNMA Optional Delivery	FNMA ARM	Jan	11.50	1000	96.550	98 550	(19,500)
	FHA VA	30	570		CONV	Feb	12.50	3000	96.995	97 667	(20,160)
	CONV	30	600								
	FHLMC	30	250								
Total			1870								
Closing in thirty days	FHA ARM	30	200								
	FNMA ARM	30	385								
	FHA VA	30	325								
	FHLMC	30	285								
	CONV	30	500								
Total			1695		Total		4000				(39,660)

to meet its commitments.[9] Similarly, out-of-the-money options may be useful in the near future, depending on price movements in the marketplace. A rise in prices may move call options into-the-money, and a drop in prices could place put options in-the-money. Therefore, the marketing staff must monitor out-of-the-money options in relation to rate movements to be aware of potential marketing opportunities.

Tracking Fallout. The current position may be used as a starting point for estimating price exposure; but in order to do so, a firm must have reliable means of measuring fallout. Most companies use historical data to derive a fallout ratio—a rough average of the percentage of applications expected not to close. Developing fallout ratios, as described in Chapter I, is not a difficult process, but historical fallout patterns will vary in relation to different interest rate cycles and other market conditions. For example, fallout can be expected to be greater during periods of decreasing interest rates as borrowers forego their "free puts" to seek a better price, and lower when rates are rising (See Exhibit 3.5). Therefore the application of fallout patterns must correlate with future expectations about interest rates.

The fallout ratio can be subgrouped by loan type, specific loan product, refinance loans, guarantee term, branch and loan officer, etc., to further improve the database for the marketing and production functions.

Future Price Risk. To measure the effect of price changes on the firm's position, data from the mark-to-market and floating at market reports may be used to calculate percentages of loans or commitments that are exposed to price risk if interest rates rise or fall. Exhibit 3.6 illustrates both short and long risk analyses based on hypothetical interest rate movements.

The Short Risk Ratio shows the percentage of the pipeline after projected fallout that must close to cover mandatory sales should prices rise. It is computed by dividing the net mandatory position by the pipeline after projected for fallout. The Long Risk Ratio shows the percentage of coverage that is currently available to protect the pipeline after adjusted for fallout if market prices

---

9   Ibid., 25.

Exhibit 3.5 Measuring Fallout: Possible Pipeline Fallout Rates (Percent Fallout vs. Security Prices at Close)

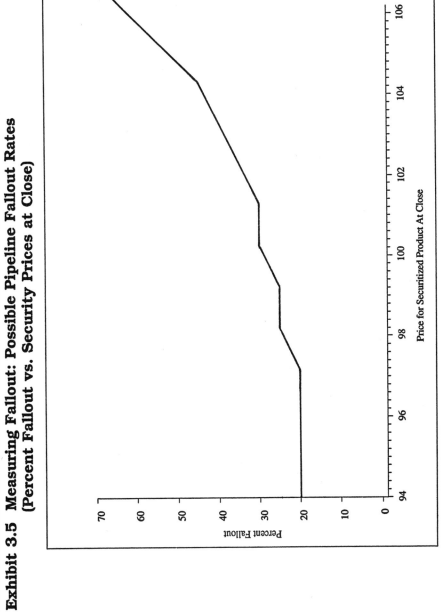

Exhibit 3.6
Market Position Risk Analysis

Short Risk Analysis: Risk of prices rising

	Plus Points			
	0	1	2	3
Net Mandatory Position	13561 Short	13561 Short	13561 Short	13561 Short
Soft Long	31695	31695	31695	31695
*Short Risk Ratio	42.79%	42.79%	42.79%	42.79%

Net Mandatory Position
divided by Soft Long

Limit: 50% Maximum
Operating Target: 30%

*Short risk ratio shows the percentage of discounted pipline that must close to cover mandatory sales.

Long Risk Analysis: Risk of prices falling

	Minus Points			
	0	1	2	3
Total Soft Long	31695	31695	31695	31695
Optional Short	0	3000	4000	4000
Net Mandatory Position	13561 Short	13561 Short	13561 Short	13561 Short
Balance to Cover Soft Soft Long: Pipeline	13561 Short	16561 Short	17561 Short	17561 Short
Net Position	18134 Long	15134 Long	14134 Long	14134 Long
*Long Risk Ratio: Balance to Cover Soft Long divided by Soft Long	42.79%	52.25%	55.41%	55.41%

Limit: 50% Minimum
Operating Target: 75%

*Long risk ratio shows the percentage of coverage that is available to protect the discounted pipeline.

were to fall. For each scenario, management should set target ratios and minimum or maximum exposure limits.[10]

If mandatory commitments exceed the pipeline/inventory and if interest rates drop (prices rise), the firm's major concern will be whether or not enough loans in the pipeline close to cover mandatory sales. Fallout will rise as borrowers choose not to close their loans at higher than market interest rates.[11] With fallout up, a firm is less likely to meet mandatory commitments, unless whole loans or securities are purchased on the open market.

If there are more pipeline/inventory loans than commitments, concern about interest rates rising (prices falling) is in order. If prices fall, the primary concern will be whether there are sufficient mandatory and optional sales to cover the pipeline. As homebuyers rush to lock in current market rates, decreasing fallout will exacerbate this risk. Profits will be maintained only if the inventory is fully covered; and pipeline gains can be achieved only if there are excess commitments.[12]

Investor Default and Exposure

The price risk associated with exposure to specific investors is often overlooked, but is nonetheless a major consideration. Management must not only consider price risk in the context of matching pipeline and inventory with commitments, but also in terms of commitment exposure to each investor. A report similar to the Investor Exposure Report in Exhibit 3.7 may be developed for this purpose.

The Investor Exposure Report measures the current total gain or loss on the aggregate, unfilled and/or unfunded commitments for each investor, as well as the current actual gain or loss for the allocated but unfunded portions of the commitments. The total gain or loss for a particular investor's commitments represents the firm's current "exposure" to that investor, or the dollar amount subject to risk of investor default.[13]

---

10 Ibid., 34.
11 Ibid., 33.
12 Ibid., 34.
13 Ibid., 36.

Exhibit 3.7 Market Position Report: Investor Exposure

Length of Contract

Investor		Mandatory Inside 4 Months A. Limit / B. Actual	Mandatory Outside 4 Months A. Limit / B. Actual	Optional Inside 4 Months A. Limit / B. Actual	Optional Outside 4 Months A. Limit / B. Actual	Outstanding Volume A. Limit / B. Actual	Deficit Exposure A. Limit / B. Actual
A G Becker	A	12,000,000	2,000,000	4,000,000	1,000,000	19,000,000	380,000
	B	5,000,000		3,000,000		8,000,000	50,285
American	A	6,000,000	1,000,000	1,000,000	1,000,000	9,000,000	201,500
	B	4,000,000		1,000,000		5,000,000	12,576
Brubaker	A	8,000,000	1,500,000	1,000,000		10,500,000	155,000
	B	4,000,000				4,000,000	21,679
First Boston	A	10,000,000	2,000,000			12,000,000	240,000
	B	7,500,000				7,500,000	(11,143)
First Federal	A	7,000,000		1,500,000		8,500,000	170,000
	B	7,000,000		1,500,000		8,500,000	0
FNMA	A	14,000,000	4,000,000	4,000,000		22,000,000	367,480
	B	7,000,000				7,000,000	0
Goldman Sachs	A	10,000,000	1,000,000			11,000,000	220,000
	B	9,000,000				9,000,000	10,980
Merrill Lynch	A	6,000,000	2,000,000	1,000,000	1,000,000	10,000,000	205,000
	B	4,000,000		1,000,000		5,000,000	0
Salomon	A	15,000,000	4,000,000	3,000,000	2,000,000	24,000,000	456,780
	B	12,000,000		2,000,000		14,000,000	32,000
Union Life	A	5,000,000		3,000,000	1,000,000	9,000,000	150,000
	B	4,000,000		2,500,000		6,500,000	0
Universal	A	5,000,000		1,000,000		6,000,000	120,000
	B	2,000,000		1,000,000		3,000,000	(9,654)
TOTALS	A	98,000,000	17,500,000	19,500,000	6,000,000	141,000,000	2,665,760
	B	65,500,000	0	12,000,000	0	77,500,000	106,723
NET AMOUNTS		32,500,000	17,500,000	7,500,000	6,000,000	63,500,000	

During periods of rising interest rates, an investor may default because of the loss in value of loan product. An investor's failure to purchase loans as agreed will erode the gains or widen the losses related to the commitment. If the investor fails its purchase obligation, a replacement commitment may need to be acquired by the firm, usually at higher prevailing market prices.

"Investor commitments can normally extend months into the future, beyond the time frame of the firm's origination cycle. Market conditions can change frequently and substantially between the time a commitment is signed and the time it is filled."[14]

Other Investor-Related Risks

Investor exposure may also be affected by product, delivery, and quality risks. In other words, profits related to commitments may be narrowed or lost and losses widened if the firm produces poor quality loans, non-conforming products, or makes late delivery or no delivery at all. However, these last three risks can result in additional costs unrelated to pure price risk. Thus, while price risk is a component of product, delivery, and quality risks, respectively, other measurement techniques must be applied to quantify and evaluate the total risk.

Product Risk. Product risk is measured by the potential opportunity cost for loans that a firm is unable to sell to investors, either because of investor default or unwillingness of the market to accept the products. In the case of investor default and where the loans comply with agency (Fannie Mae, Freddie Mac, and FHA/VA) requirements, the exposure may be limited to the price risk so far discussed. However, in the case of non-conforming products, the risks are greatly amplified due to the lack of liquidity or a significant number of willing buyers and sellers for that type of product.

In the case of jumbo loans or those exceeding a loan size Fannie Mae and Freddie Mac are allowed to purchase, a yield premium of 37.5 to 50 basis points is typically demanded by most

---

14 Ibid., 37.

investors. Deviating from standard secondary market requirements and producing loans without permanent takeout commitments is unqualified speculation.

Product risk is difficult, if not impossible to quantify accurately. Considering that the typical firm is highly leveraged and reuses the same capital many times a year to generate warehousing spreads, fee income, and servicing revenues, the potential cost or product risk is quite high. Restricted capital will affect the lender's ability to borrow, resulting in reduced warehousing spreads and lost profits for the period of time that the firm must carry the loans on its books.

Delivery Risk. Similar to product risk, the risk of owning an unsalable product because of an error or delay in delivery equals the cost of effecting ultimate delivery, plus price risk and the opportunity cost of the money spent to fund the problematic loan in the interim. Late delivery may result in penalty fees, forfeiture of interest, repurchase or substitution, or pairing off trades. If an investor rejects loans outright due to late delivery, the opportunity cost of carrying the loans longer than anticipated can translate into reduced warehousing spreads and lost profits.

All of these aforementioned costs can be estimated from historical data, and some may even be measured prospectively. The penalty may be forfeited interest cost, a dollar amount based on then current market conditions and repurchase may be required at the higher of par or the funding price. (If the loans were sold in a Ginnie Mae pool for less than par, a loss is immediately incurred because repurchase at par is required.)

In addition to tracking the number of late deliveries and the costs of penalty fees, forfeited interest, repurchases, pair-offs, and opportunity costs, delivery risk may be measured indirectly by how far below optimal efficiency levels a firm's staff is working. Inadequate staffing and/or low productivity can be a primary cause of delivery problems.

Quality. Quality risk is measured by the cost of making unsound loans as a result of non-conformance in investor and insurer disclosure, underwriting, appraisal, and documentation requirements. These costs take shape in the form of repurchases, rejected insurance claims, lost interest on advances to mortgage pools, unpaid principal and interest payments on repurchased loans, and collection and foreclosure expenses. All of these costs can be measured at least historically and may serve as a guide for estimating future expenditures.

A second method for measuring quality risk is to track 'delinquencies and foreclosures. Management must continually track the number, percentages, and status of delinquent loans and loans-in-foreclosure so that an unusually high percentage of these loans can be noted, investigated, and remedial steps put in place. Delinquency ratios should be tracked and compared with both historical trends of the company itself and those of the nation, region, or state. By tracking delinquency ratios and trends, a company can estimate what its future exposure will be, taking into consideration its projected loan volume and other pertinent factors.

Intra-company ratios are most useful if they are categorized by loan type, branch office, and loan officer, which will allow management to focus on particular sources for high level delinquencies. In making national, state, or regional comparisons, a quarterly delinquency survey published by the Mortgage Bankers Association of America (MBA) may be used. The MBA delinquency report classifies loans by state and region, the number of days delinquent, and foreclosures started during the quarter.

Another, less direct method for assessing quality risk is to keep track of the number, kinds, and sources of errors and omissions made by the firm's staff. To avoid unforeseen losses and to comply with new investor requirements, many firms conduct a continual internal audit inspection of randomly-selected closed loan files that are current in their obligations. If the results of these audits list all errors and discrepancies, including missing documents, improper calculations, or inadequate disclosures, management can assess the quality risk relative to its loan production operation.

Quantifying External Risk

The external risks are market driven and beyond the firm's control. Market movement can be directed by behavior patterns, policies, legislation, and historical patterns. Each influence must be analyzed and its impact on the overall market performance assessed.

Measuring Interest Rate Trends and Volatility

There are two general approaches to evaluating and forecasting interest rate movements: these include (1) a fundamental analysis of the supply and demand for credit based on the state of the economy and related factors or events; and (2) the application of technical analysis, statistics, probability, or other mathematical techniques to historical data in efforts to anticipate future trends. Generally, technical analysis and other mathematical techniques are objective methods that are used to supplement the more subjective fundamental analysis of the economy.

As interest rate volatility has increased over the past few years, so has the frustration of solely using traditional methods of fundamental analysis. Fundamental analysis is concerned with the many economic and financial factors that affect supply and demand. Technical analysis is only concerned with the study of prices and their mathematical relationships. The technician reasons that all fundamental knowledge makes itself known as prices, so that is all that one needs to study. There are very few pure fundamentalists or pure technicians; as indicated, most market analysts consider both areas to derive their marketing conclusions.

Fundamental Analysis of the Economy

Four broad areas influence the supply and demand for credit, which in turn cause interest rate volatility—(1) the state of the domestic economy; (2) policies and action of the Federal Reserve Board and the U.S. Treasury; (3) foreign capital flows; and (4) U.S. Congressional legislation and proposals. While each of these areas may be considered separately, they are in fact interrelated and each one influences and is influenced by the others.

The Domestic Economy. The state of the economy often dictates the level of demand for money and credit; liquidity and interest rates reflect that demand. When the economy is expanding, demand for credit increases and interest rates usually rise. If the economy is slowing or recessionary, interest rates usually fall. The Commerce and Treasury Departments and other institutions provide clues to the state of the economy each month in the form of releases containing information and analyses of major economic indicators. Historical information and projections of upcoming releases are available from the U.S. Treasury, brokerage houses, and business publications.

The major economic indicators are shown in Exhibit 3.8, which contains for each one an approximate release date, a general evaluation of its relative importance in affecting the economy, its key components, and important information used to forecast indicator values. The general impact of some of these indicators on the direction of interest rates is illustrated in Exhibit 3.9.

Obviously, a fundamental analysis of all of this data relative to the economy and interest rates is a complex task, far beyond the scope of this book. Economists will disagree as to the importance of each indicator, forecasts of future activity, modeling techniques, and the actual values that may be derived from such forecasts. Management should be aware of this complexity and the need for expert advice in structuring production and marketing strategies based on economic expectations.

The Federal Reserve. The Federal Reserve System is the central bank of the United States. Among other responsibilities the Federal Reserve sets and executes monetary policy which in turn affects interest rate volatility. The Board implements monetary policy through the coordinated use of three instruments—open market operations, the regulation of member bank discounting with Federal Reserve banks, and changes in member bank reserve requirements. All three instruments affect the availability of bank reserves, money, and the cost of credit generally.[15]

Through its open market operations, the central bank purchases and sells securities, mainly U.S. Government securities such as Treasury bills, in the over-the-counter market. In general, aggregate trading in the U.S. Government securities market averages billions of dollars a day, and the market is by far the broadest and most active of the U.S. financial markets. When the Federal Reserve buys securities, the supply of bank reserves is expanded, and when it sells, reserve availability contracts.

---

15 For a full discussion of monetary policy and execution, see *The Federal Reserve System—Purposes and Functions, Sixth Edition*, Board of Governors of the Federal Reserve System, Washington, D.C. (September 1974).

Exhibit 3.8

Release	Approx. Date	Importance	Affects	Key Components	Forecast Tools
Construction Spending	1st	Low	- GNP	- Residential - Non-residential - Public	- Tax law changes - Weather
Employment	5th	High	- Ind. Prod. - Pers. Income - GNP	- Non-farm breakdown - Hours worked - Earnings data	- Initial claims - Strikes - Seasonal factors
Consumer Credit	7th	Med.	- Leaders	- Auto credit	- Auto incentives
Wholesale Trade	10th	Low	- GNP	- Invt./Sales ratio	
PPI	11th	High	- CPI	- Capital equip. - Food - Energy	- Oil prices - Auto incentives - Agricultural Prices
Retail Sales	13th	Med.	- PCE	- Auto sales	- Auto incentives - Gas/Food prices - Dep. store sales
Business Inventories	13th	Low	- GNP	- Invt./Sales ratio	- Manuf., whole-sale data prev. released
Trade Balance	14th	High	- GNP - Dollar	- Manufacturing - Agricultural - Petroleum	

Exhibit 3.8 (Continued)

Release	Approx. Date	Importance	Affects	Key Components	Forecast Tools
Industrial Production	15th	High	- Capacity utilization - GNP	- Auto assemblies	- Weather - Strikes - Manufacturing Emp. - Manufacturing Hours
Housing Starts	18th	Med.	- Leaders	- Single unit - Multiple unit	- Permits - Weather
GNP	19th	High		- Final sales - Inventories	
Personal Income	20th	Med.	- GNP	- Wages/Salaries - Farm/Non-farm Inc.	- Subsidies/Payments - Earnings data
Durable Goods	23rd	High	- GNP - Factory orders	- Defense - Non-defense capital goods	- Aircraft orders
CPI	23rd	High	- Leaders	- Energy - Food - Housing	- Oil prices - Auto incentives - Food (PPI)
Leading Indicators	29th	Med.		- Stock prices - M2	- Prior data for most series
New Home Sales	30th	Low		- Houses for sale at end of period	- Weather - Tax law changes
Agricultural Prices	30th	Low	- PPI		- Commodity prices
Factory Orders	31st	Low	- GNP	- Durables - Non-durables	- Durables orders

Prepared for Mortgage Bankers Association Conference, Kansas City, March 25-27, 1987.
Fundamental Factors in Risk Management, by Richard C. Green, Chairman, Money Market Services, Inc.

Exhibit 3.9

Inflation Expectation Indicators	Factor Trend	Components	Interest Rate Impact	Bond Reason/Effect
1) Unemployment	Up	Nonseasonal Non-Farm New claims	Down	Slowing economy
2) Consumer Price Index (CPI)	Up	Consumer goods; Food, clothing, fuel prices, etc.	Up	Inflationary rates up
3) Producer Price Index (PPI)	Up	Prices of goods, such as raw materials	Up	Investors require higher rates of return
Business Indications				
4) Housing Starts	Up	Building Permits	Up	Economy growing; housing demand may drive rates up
5) Personal Income	Up	Personal earnings Non-farm	Up	The higher the income the consumption increases; demand increases supply
6) Retail Sales	Up	Auto Sales Dept. Store Sales	Up	Increased consumer spending up—Economy growing
7) Leading Indicators	Up	Various	Up	Strong growing economy
8) Industrial Production	Down	Amount of goods produced	Down	Slowing of economic growth
9) Business Inventories	Up	Factory wholesale inventories	Down	Absorption *not* keeping up with production—Economy slowing
10) Durable/Factory Goods Orders	Up	Non-Defense Capital Spending	Up	Strong demand—Economy growing

In situations where the central bank wants to make temporary additions to bank reserves, it engages in short-term repurchase agreements (repos) with dealers. This permits an injection of reserves for a short period, after which the reserves will automatically be drawn back when the repos mature. Conversely, when the central bank faces a temporary need to absorb rather than provide bank reserves, it employs sale-purchase (reverse repo) transactions.

Through its discount window, the Federal Reserve regulates the cost at which member banks may borrow from the central bank. Member banks borrow from the Federal Reserve for short periods of time, usually no more than a few days, as they seek to make temporary adjustments in their reserves. These borrowing needs are brought about by unexpected increases in loan demand, sudden deposit losses, and temporary difficulties in banks' ability to obtain funds from other money market sources.

The interest rate the Federal Reserve charges to member banks directly affects the rates that the banks charge on loans to their customers, thereby affecting interest rate levels in general. An increase in the discount rate will lead directly to an increase in the prime rate, and vice versa.

Within prescribed limits, the Federal Reserve has the authority to regulate reserve requirements for its member banks by setting minimum ratios for the reserves against demand and time deposits. These limits range from three to 14 percent on demand deposits and from zero to nine percent on time deposits. Changes in reserve requirements are normally designed to help moderate inflationary or recessionary tendencies in the economy.

Even a small change in a required reserve ratio may have a large potential impact on deposits and bank credit nationwide. Adjustments in reserve ratios and discount rates are used less frequently than open market operations to adjust reserves. Open market operations are unannounced; thus, there is no announcement effect on the credit markets if the same amount of reserve changes are made through open market transactions. In addition, the impact of open market operations, unlike the other two instruments, tends to be gradual, concentrated first on large money center banks and filtering subsequently to smaller and more remotely located banks.

By tracking data on money supply, bank reserve growth, and federal funds targeting, it is possible to ascertain hints as to whether the Federal Reserve might be tightening or easing interest rates. When money is plentiful, interest rates usually fall and vice versa. Exhibit 3.10 illustrates the impact on interest rate trends when the central bank uses its instruments of monetary policy.

The U.S. Treasury. The U.S. Treasury is responsible for borrowing to finance the federal debt. The agency borrows by issuing securities in the form of Treasury bills, notes, and bonds. These borrowings are of two types— (1) cash borrowings, which raise new money and expand the size of the outstanding public debt; and (2) refinancings, which roll over outstanding debt into new issues as it matures.

As federal deficits have increased dramatically in the past decade, the structure and timing of Treasury auctions has had an increasing impact on interest rate volatility. This is due primarily to the sheer size and growth of the deficit and the required borrowings, as well as the marketing advantage that the Treasury has over other borrowers because of the "full faith and credit" backing of the U.S. Government for its securities.

Therefore, the U.S. Treasury enjoys a preferred status as a borrower in the securities market. Large Treasury auctions tend to absorb much of the funds available for credit in the securities market, thereby "crowding out" many borrowers and causing higher interest rates to be charged for the remaining funds for which there is a relatively higher demand.

These large scale Treasury financings may occur over a period extending from one to three weeks. Depending on market conditions and attitudes at the time, wide swings in interest rates have sometimes occurred during, immediately preceding, and following these financings. Market analysts must therefore consider the impact of pending Treasury auctions in light of Federal Reserve policies and the general availability of credit in assessing interest rate volatility. Exhibit 3.11 describes the auction cycles for both discount and coupon Treasury securities.

Foreign Capital Flows. Persistent trade surpluses by our international trading partners, notably Japan and West Germany, have made our domestic economy more dependent on foreign capital (U.S. dollars held by foreign governments and financial institutions) to finance our trade deficits. In addition, more of this

Exhibit 3.10

Fed Policy	Impact	Reason
Fed raises the discount rate. (This is the rate at which member banks of the Federal Reserve can borrow from the Fed's discount window.)	Up	An increase in interest rates between banks and the Fed usually means that an increase in rates to customers follows. This action is used to slow credit expansion.
Money supply figures are up. (M1 = the total of private demand, or checking account deposits, at commercial banks plus cash in public hands. M2 = everything in M1 plus savings accounts, individual money market mutual fund accounts and certain other bank borrowings. M3 = M2 plus larger time deposits, institutional money markets mutual fund accounts and certain other bank borrowings.)	Up	Excess growth in money supply causes inflation and generates fears that the Fed may tighten reserve growth by allowing the Fed funds rate to rise.
Fed does Repo's.	Down	The Fed puts money into the banking system by purchasing collateral and agreeing to resell later. This increase in bank reserves may bring rates down.
Fed does Reserves or Matched Sales (Reverse repo's).	Up	The Fed takes money from the system by selling collateral and agreeing to repurchase the same at a later date. This decrease in bank reserves generally pushes interest rates up.
Fed buys bills.	Down	The Fed adds reserves to the banking system. This increase in reserves may cause interest rates to drop.

Exhibit 3.11   Treasury Auction Cycles

Discount securities:

Three-month (91-day) Treasury bills	Auctioned every Monday; issued on the following Thursday.
Six-month (182-day) Treasury bills	Same auction and issue cycle as for three-month Treasury bills (auctioned on Monday; issued on Thursday). Thus, 182-day Treasury bills eventually trade in consonance with 91-day Treasury bills.
Fifty-two week (364-day) Treasury bills	Auctioned every fourth Thursday; issued on the following Thursday. Thus, 364-day Treasury bills eventually trade in consonance with 182-day and then 91-day Treasury bills.

Coupon securities:

Two-year	Two-year Treasury notes are auctioned every month, normally near the end of the month, for settlement on the last business day of the month and mature on the last business day of the month two years hence.
Five-year	Five-year Treasury notes are auctioned on a quarterly cycle near the end of the February, May, August and November months for settlement at the beginning of the March, June, September and December months. These issues mature on the 15th of the February, May, August and November months approximately five years and two months after their settlement date (these notes are, thus, five-year, two-month notes and their first coupon is a long coupon, that is, the first coupon represents approximately eight months interest).
Mini-Refunding (Four-year/seven-year)	The mini-refunding is a quarterly cycle issue of, typically, a four-year note, and a seven-year note. These issues are announced at the same time, typically during the middle of the auction month. They are then typically auctioned on consecutive business days late during the March, June, September and December months for settlement at the beginning of the January, April, July and October months. The four-year note matures on the last business day of the March, June, September, and December months four years after settlement; the seven-year note matures on the 15th day of the January, April, July and October months seven years after settlement.
Refunding (Three-year/ten-year/thirty-year	The refunding cycle is a quarterly cycle issue of notes and bonds which are issued on the 15th day of the February, May, August and November quarterly cycle months and are typically auctioned on Tuesday, Wednesday and Thursday during the second week prior to the issue. Each refunding typically contains three issues: (1) a 3-year note, (2) a 10-year note, and (3) a 30-year bond. These issues mature on the 15th day of the February, May, August or November months, the appropriate number of years (3, 10 or 30) after their issue. The issues in the refunding cycle have, however, been subject to some variations.
Summary of Maturity Schedule	15th day of February, May, August and November months: 3-year; 5-year; 10-year; and 30-year.
	15th day of January, April, July, and October: 7-year
	End of Month: 2-year (monthly); 4-year (March, June, September, and December).

foreign capital has found its way into the U.S. Treasury debt market, the stock market, and real estate markets. It is estimated that more than 20 percent of all U.S. Treasury securities trading is done by foreigners.

A burgeoning trade deficit can affect the overall growth of the economy, the rate of inflation, and interest rates.[16] Therefore, when considering the state of the economy and the direction in which it is headed, it is necessary to factor in the increasingly significant effect of foreign cash flows. One way to measure the potential effect of foreign cash flows is to track changes in the value of the dollar in the exchange markets.

An exchange rate change has both fiscal and monetary effects; it directly affects both prices and aggregate demand for goods and services, thereby having a direct effect also on real money balances. For example, a rise in the exchange rate reduces real GNP growth through its effect on the relative prices of imports and exports, which is the "fiscal" effect of appreciation in the dollar. However, since such appreciation in the dollar tends also to lower the average level of prices, it increases real money balances. Similarly, a reduction in the exchange rate may have opposite effects. Thus, exchange rate changes can have a bearing on the cyclical movements of some significant economic and financial variables.[17]

Many economists believe that increases in the exchange rate have two principal causes—(1) widening differentials between U.S. and foreign real interest rates, and (2) shifts in asset preferences toward dollar-denominated claims due to substantially higher U.S. real interest rates relative to foreign rates. Thus, a rise in real interest rates on U.S. financial assets in relation to those abroad may be a powerful stimulant for inflows of foreign capital.[18] Changes in the differentials between U.S. and foreign real interest rates may therefore be precursors of future exchange rate changes.

The above of course is a simplified explanation of a very complex topic. In practice, economists and financial analysts measure

---

16 Gramley, Lyle E., "The Effects of Exchange Rate Changes on the U.S. Economy," *Business Economics* (July 1985).

17 Ibid.

18 Ibid.

the effect of exchange rate changes through the use of sophisticated models involving other significant variables and differing assumptions and techniques.

The U.S. Congress. Actions by the U.S. Congress in proposing or passing legislation, or acquiescence by the Congress in certain circumstances, can have a great influence upon the economy and interest rates. For example, the probability that Congress will or will not pass legislation that will substantially reduce the current federal budget deficit may have significant short- and long-term implications for the credit markets. A sizable reduction in the deficit could directly reduce the influence and activity of the U.S. Treasury in the securities markets, as well as cause some fundamental changes in the direction of the economy and in the policies of the Federal Reserve Board. On the other hand, procrastination by Congress in moving toward a balanced budget would signal sustained or increased activity by the Treasury in the credit markets.

Furthermore, particular changes in federal tax laws, trade laws and regulations, laws governing broad industries or commodities, and other economic legislation can have a profound impact on the expectations of investors, and consequently on yields required by securities markets. The probability that changes in government laws or regulations will result in diminished rates of return for investors is a political risk that is often difficult, if not impossible, to measure. However, the experienced analyst can anticipate and forecast general trends in the economy or the credit markets that may be caused by specific legislation pending before Congress.

Technical Analysis

While a fundamental analysis of the economy deals primarily with the factors affecting interest rate trends, technical analysis is concerned with studying the action of the interest rate market itself. If the analysis were confined solely to fundamental factors, the risk of miscalculation would be greater because many financial and economic indicators are not easily quantified for timing purposes. As a result, an interest rate peak or trough may arrive earlier or later than the fundamental analysis indicates. For this reason, technical analysis, which provides more specific signals of interest rate peaks and valleys through objective measurement, may be used to supplement fundamental analysis.[19]

Many technical analysis methods are used to study the interest rate markets. Commonly used methods include: moving average, relative strength, Elliot Wave Analysis, Fibonnaci relationships, time cycle studies, stochastics, pivot points, point and figure charting, bar chart formations, and Gann squares and lines. The most familiar form of technical analysis though is the moving average, which has been used to evaluate securities price trends for years.

Technical methods are generally considered as trend-following or non-trending. A trend-following system enables a firm to establish a long or short position after a price trend has been established. A non-trending system is used to make a trace within the boundaries of an established trading range. Most technical analysis methods, however, are trend-following systems.

Basic trend analysis involves the recognition of price patterns, the direction of price trends, potential changes in direction, and the rate of change or momentum of trends. The following discussion of trend analysis is intended only to familiarize the reader with some of these basic concepts and their implications.[20]

Identifying Price Patterns. In its basic state, the primary objective of technical analysis is to isolate a price trend and employ a method to identify the reversal of the trend at an early stage. By plotting price points over time and fitting curves to those points, the technical analyst can discern certain distinct trends and patterns. A price trend is the direction that prices of the financial instrument are moving over time, either up, down, or horizontal. Within the trend or cycle, certain recognizable patterns or formations may be formed, as shown in the figures comprising Exhibit 3.12.

---

19 Pring, Martin J., *How to Forecast Interest Rates,* McGraw-Hill Book Company (1981): 141.
20 For a complete discussion on this subject, see Martin J. Pring, *How to Forecast Interest Rates* (1982), Chapter Twelve.

Exhibit 3.12

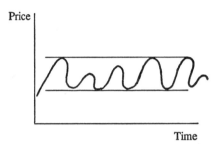

Figure 1

Figure 2

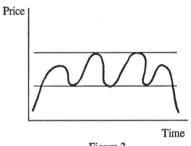

Figure 3

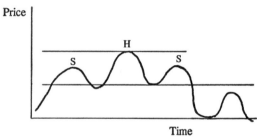

Figure 4

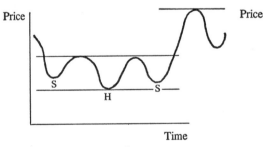

Figure 5

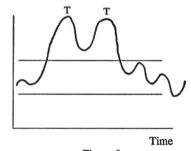

Figure 6

Exhibit 3.12 (Continued)

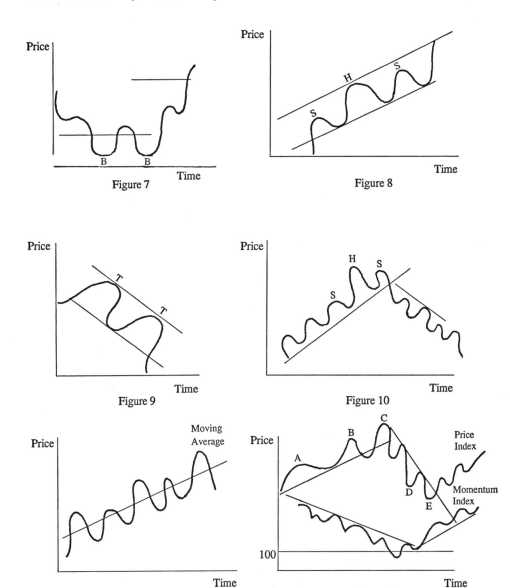

Figure 7

Figure 8

Figure 9

Figure 10

Figure 11

Figure 12

For example, the formation shown in Figure 1 of Exhibit 3.12 is called a rectangle because the price movements are, for a period, confined between two distinct parallel boundaries. When prices move outside of those boundaries, a breakout has occurred, which may signal that a new trend has emerged. A breakout that is opposite the previous trend is known as a reverse pattern, and one that is consistent with the previous trend is a continuation pattern. Reverse and continuation patterns are shown in Figures 2 and 3, respectively. A rectangle can occur either at the bottom or at the top of a price or interest rate cycle.

A simple head and shoulders pattern (Figure 4) consists of a head, the final rally, separated by two smaller rallies, the left and right shoulders. The right shoulder in the example is actually the first rally of a declining trend, which is signalled by a break in the neckline, the line joining the base of the two shoulders. An inverse head and shoulders pattern is shown in Figure 5. A head and shoulders pattern can also contain more than one shoulder on either side of the head.

A double top formation (Figure 6) consists of two rallies separated by a reaction, followed by a decline below the reaction line. A double bottom formation, shown in Figure 7, is the opposite of a double top formation. The reversal in each example is signalled when the price moves below or above the reaction line, respectively. All of these formations can develop on either rising or falling lines as shown in Figures 8 and 9. Over the years, experienced analysts have identified many other common formations similar to the ones just discussed.

Of utmost importance is the size of a price pattern, which is measured by the length of time before it is completed and the distance between its high and low points. For example, a formation that develops over the course of one or two weeks may not actually signal a peak or trough in the cycle, whereas one that develops over the course of several months will almost certainly signal that the peak or trough has been reached. The analyst must therefore be aware of whipsaws, which appear at first to be breakouts but are in fact only misleading movements. Criteria to minimize or filter out whipsaws must then be established.

Trendiness. To establish the direction of a price cycle and its length, a simple trendline may be constructed. As shown in Figure 10, a trendline is drawn along the bottom of the troughs for rising patterns and along the top of the peaks of falling patterns. If the price pattern or price index crosses the trendline, it may be an indication of trend reversal. Similarly, if the price index falls away from the trendline, it may indicate a continuation, up or down. In either case, the possibility of a whipsaw also exists. When a breakout from a pattern and a crossover of the trendline occur at the same time however, it is a stronger indication that a reversal has occurred.[21]

The number of times a trendline is touched by the price index, the steepness of the trendline, and the trendline length is of primary importance. The greater the number of times a trendline is touched by the peaks or troughs of the price index, the greater the confirmation of the direction of the trend. Therefore, if the price index crosses a trendline that it has touched several or more times, it is a stronger indication of a trend reversal.

Generally, a sharply steeper trendline represents a trend that is less likely to be sustained. A break of the steep trendline by the price index has a higher likelihood of indicating a continuation of the trend in the same but less steep direction. Reversals after significantly long trends often result in the new trend being comparatively lengthy.[22]

Moving Averages. A moving average may be used to recognize the point at which a reversal may occur earlier than would be indicated by breaks of the trendline, in addition to quantifying the direction of the price trend. A simple moving average is constructed by averaging prices for a number of consecutive periods and recalculating the average in each new period for the same number of consecutive periods. For example, a five-day moving average where the prices on each day were 94, 95, 96, 96.5, and 97, respectively, would have an initial value of 95.7 (478.5 divided by 5).

On the sixth day, a new price for that day would be included in the calculation and the first day's price would be dropped. Therefore, if the price for the sixth day is 98, the moving average would change to 96.5 (482.5 divided by 5). This process is repeated each new day so that the average "moves." This moving average

---

21 Ibid., 148.
22 Ibid.

may be plotted in relation to the actual price movements, or price index, as shown in Figure 11.

When the price index crosses the moving average, either up or down, a reversal of the trend may be indicated. However, if the price index crosses the moving average while the average is still moving in the same direction, the possibility of a whipsaw is high even though the break may still indicate a potential reversal. Confirmation of the trend reversal is obtained when the moving average itself changes direction. However, if the price index crosses the moving average when the average is flat or has already changed direction, it is a strong indication that a reversal has occurred.[23]

Of course, moving averages can be calculated over any time period — days, weeks, or months. However, the greater the time period, the longer the trend that is being monitored. Penetration by the price index will become more significant as the trend lengthens.[24]

Rate of Change. A rate of change or momentum index may be used to measure the rate at which interest rates or prices change over any period of time. To construct a simple momentum index relating to a price index for a particular period—20 days for example—the price recorded on the twentieth day is divided by the price recorded 20 days ago. The price recorded on each succeeding day is then divided by the price recorded 20 days before and so on. These values are typically set to an index of 100 and plotted in the same manner as price points are, usually just below the price index on the same graph (Figure 12).

A rising rate of change index implies growth in momentum, and a falling index implies a loss in momentum. As indicated by the calculation above, momentum is measured by the amount of change in the rate or price from one period to another. An index that never changed in price would therefore be plotted as a straight line along the 100 reference line.

When the momentum index is above the reference line, the value of the price index is always higher than the previous reading even though the momentum index may be declining. Similarly,

---

23 Ibid., 151.
24 Ibid.

when the momentum index falls below the reference line, the price index at that point is always lower than the previous reading. Typically, momentum is at its greatest at or near a cyclical trough, after which the momentum index and the price index may diverge. Divergence occurs because the price index may rally even higher, though at a loss of momentum (note points B and C in Figure 12).

A divergence of the two indexes is a preliminary indication of possible trend reversal. Since the divergence may occur early in a price pattern due to greater momentum at that point, it is essential to wait confirmation of the reversal. Confirmation may be obtained by: (1) the penetration of an important trendline, as shown in Figure 12; (2) the crossover of a moving average; and/or (3) a breakout from the price pattern.[25]

When the momentum index peaks simultaneously with the price index (Figure 13), it provides no advance warning of an imminent reversal. However, the weakness of the trend and possible reversal may be indicated again by penetration of the trendline or the moving average, or by a price pattern breakout.

Exhibits 3.13 and 3.14 illustrate how technical analysis methods are applied to actual rate or price data. Hopefully, this discussion and the examples have given the reader at least a flavor of technical analysis. In practice, technical analysts employ a combination of computerized models that range from the simple to the very complex, often incorporating fundamental economic variables as well as trading objectives and activities. Although the moving average is the most well-known technique employed, it is rarely used alone; rather, it is used in conjunction with other more complex technical methods, as well as with probability, statistics, and other mathematical techniques.

Automated systems designed for pattern recognition are plentiful. These systems can search a database and calculate the number of times a particular pattern has led to a certain result. Other systems are designed to analyze market movements and formulate counter moves that protect the analyst's market position. Still other systems can develop situations by pattern recognition and

---

25 Ibid., 153.

Exhibit 3.13

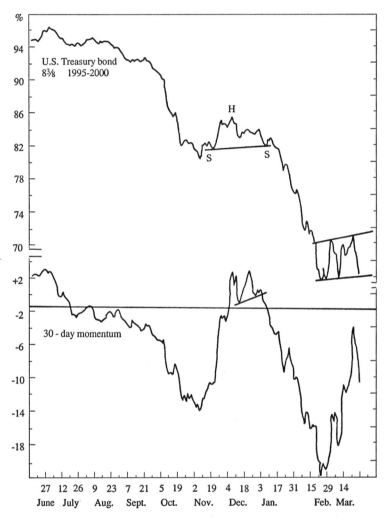

U.S. Treasury bonds 8 3/8 percent, 1995-2000. *(Interest Rate Forecast.)*

Source: Pring, Martin J., *How to Forecast Interest Rates*, McGraw-Hill, Inc., 1981.

Exhibit 3.14

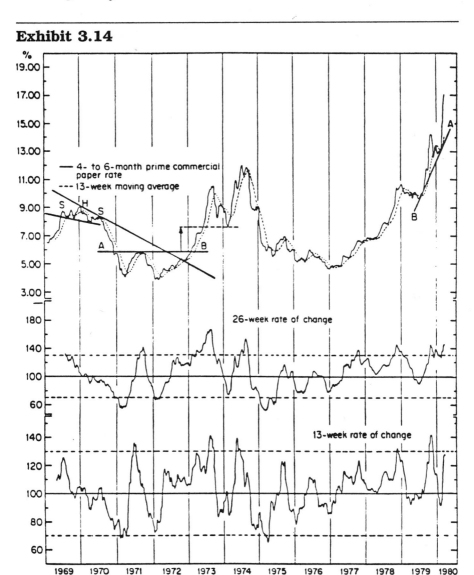

Four- to six-month commercial paper rate, 1969–1980, showing how the 1966–1969 bear market in short-term interest rates was terminated by a downward-sloping head-and-shoulder pattern. The 1972–1974 bear market, on the other hand, developed from a double bottom, the first occurring in early 1971 and the second at the beginning of 1972. A rise in rates above the dashed line *AB* was the signal that the double bottom had been completed. While the upside objective of about 7.9 percent was easily exceeded, this point proved to be the reversal point for the decline in late 1973 and early 1974. (*Interest Rate Forecast.*)

Source: Pring, Martin J., *How to Forecast Interest Rates*, McGraw-Hill, Inc., 1981.

project peaks, troughs, or breakout points. Computer applications exist that test the relative effectiveness of moving averages, the probability of extreme price movements, the nature of variations of prices around a trend, the changes in speed at different price levels, the characteristics of bull and bear markets, and countless other measurements. Clearly, technical analysis can indeed be a complex endeavor.[26]

Other Technical Considerations. Some activities associated with technical analysis may cause price movements to occur in the absence of fundamental causes, as has been true in the past few years. Examples of these technical factors would include basis trading, portfolio insurance, and the triggering of option writing programs. In all three cases, when the relationship of two different markets gets out of line by more than a predetermined amount, trades are automatically executed. This automatic trading has definitely increased volatility in ways that are not totally understood.

Statistical Measurement of Volatility

The price/volatility relationship is one of the basic aspects of price or interest rate movements. Several important characteristics of this relationship have been demonstrated over time. First, as the price level of an instrument or commodity increases, the amount by which price fluctuates can also be expected to increase because there is more latitude for fluctuations. Second, the potential for price variation will increase as the time interval used for measurement increases.

Volatility, the difference between the highest and lowest price during a time period, will likely be substantially greater over one week as opposed to one day. Volatility can be expected to increase rapidly as the time interval moves from one day to one month; but as the interval continues to increase in size, volatility will at some point reach a maximum and level off.[27]

---

26 Kaufman, Perry J., *Technical Analysis in Commodities*, John Wiley and Sons, Inc. (1980).
27 Ibid., 100-101.

Thus, there is some positive correlation among price level, the time period for measurement, and potential price fluctuations. This correlation provides some advantages in analyzing price volatility. First, by knowing the likelihood of a potential price movement at certain price levels and over specific time periods, a firm can more readily identify the risk of carrying a cash or futures position. In addition, sharp increases or decreases in price that extend beyond the probable range of volatility can be readily identified and even used to the advantage of the firm because the price can be expected, in most instances, to return to its normal range of volatility.[28]

Probability and statistical analysis is used most often to measure price volatility. More specifically, the distribution of the closing prices for a particular time period can be studied in relation to deviations from the mean price of the period. The variation is expressed as a standard deviation, which in turn is used to estimate the probability of future price fluctuations.

Volatility is often annualized and is always expressed as a percentage. For example, if a financial instrument has a 10 percent volatility, it means that over the next year the instrument's price could fluctuate by 10 percent with the probability of one standard deviation. Thus, a GNMA eight percent 30-year security priced at 90 with 10 percent volatility would fluctuate in price between 81 and 99 (90 price × .10 volatility = +/-9 points).

There are two types of volatility—historic and implied. Historic volatility is computed over a time period (20 or 40 days for example) using closing prices. Implied volatility is computed by taking an existing interest rate option and using an options pricing model solved backwards to figure the volatility implied by the option.

Mortgage bankers have become painfully aware of volatility, which has increased dramatically in recent years. Entirely different marketing strategies apply to volatility rising versus volatility falling. Keeping daily records of volatility and trying to figure why it changes enhances an understanding of marketing risk.

---

28 Ibid.

The Yield Curve

One of the most widely watched and published interest rate measurements is what is commonly known as the "yield curve." The yield curve measures the relationships between the yields on short-, medium-, and long-term debt instruments. In normal economic times, yields increase as the maturity of the debt instrument lengthens; market investors require additional yield to compensate for the risks associated with longer maturities.

Exhibit 3.15 shows a comparison of the yield curves of U.S. Treasury securities for October 15, 1979 and October 15, 1987. The 1987 yield curve is the typical relationship wherein rates on short-term maturities are lower than those on longer-term instruments. The 1979 plot shows an unusual inverted yield curve with rates on short-term maturities substantially higher than those on longer-term maturities.

Aside from the arbitrage opportunities provided for securities issuers and investors, the yield curve is also a relatively simple measurement of the liquidity pressures on the supply and demand for money. Generally, the level of interest rates is affected by the amount of liquidity in the financial system. The movement of interest rates is determined in a large part by the rate of change of liquidity; that is, the speed at which the money supply/demand relationship changes.[29]

A significant factor affecting the shape of the yield curve is current or expected Federal Reserve Board policy. When rates on shorter maturities move above those on longer maturities, it usually signals a period of financial squeeze and higher overall interest rate levels followed by a subsequent steep drop in rates—what occurred in the extreme in 1979. Conversely, when rates on shorter-term maturities move below those on longer-term instruments, easier money prevails. The economy usually responds by expanding and thus generally causing interest rates to rise.

---

29 Pring, Martin J. *How to Forecast Interest Rates*, McGraw-Hill Book Company (1981): 103.

Exhibit 3.15 Treasury Yield Curves

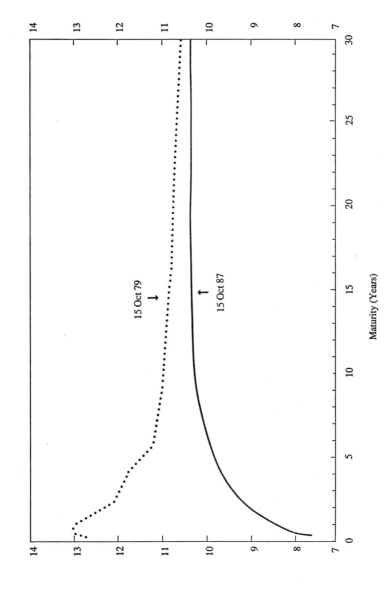

Source: Comments on Credit, Salomon Brothers Inc., October 16, 1987.

Other important factors influencing the shape of the yield curve include: (1) bullish or bearish moves in the bond market; (2) extraordinary activity in the market by various institutions such as money market mutual funds and commercial banks; (3) abrupt supply and demand imbalances that may occur even during periods of stable monetary policy; and (4) coupon disparities among issues comprising the yield curve.[30]

---

30 Fabozzi, *The Handbook of Treasury Securities Trading and Portfolio Strategies,* Probus Publishing Company (1987): 186–195.

4

Practical
Applications
of Hedging

Using the hedging tools described in Chapter 2 to protect against changes in interest rates is an imperfect science because hedging instruments introduce their own inherent risks. In addition, deciding how and when to hedge depends on a firm's assessment of the direction and volatility of interest rates, its willingness to assume risk, and the estimated costs of various strategies.

This chapter begins by showing what would happen under different conditions if a firm were to cover all of its pipeline expected to close with only one of the hedging methods. This approach is used to depict the strengths and weaknesses of each method along with the mechanics of hedging. These hedging methods also set the groundwork for integrated strategies reviewed later in the chapter.

In all of the examples, a position covering the guaranteed pipeline is established and maintained until the guarantees expire and a certain number of loans close. In the interim (60 days) this position is not altered to reflect changing market conditions, so the resulting losses and gains posted are most likely either too high or too low. (In the scenario outlining the use of futures, for example, changes in the basis are described but not counteracted with either the selling or buying of more futures contracts.) Realistically, a hedging position would be adjusted daily to compensate for an adverse market and to take advantage of a favorable one. This cannot be accomplished without the constant tracking and updating of marketing results (see Chapter 5, "Marketing Management").

The following market conditions are the ground rules and apply to all scenarios in this chapter, unless otherwise stated:

In mid-June, FNMA 9.5s are at 97:24/32 (the colon henceforth symbolizes 32nds). A firm has issued $1 million in commitment letters to make ten percent conventional loans at 2.25 discount points or a price of 97.24. The commitments are for 60 days, and 80 percent of the pipeline is expected to close. The loans can be securitized into 9.5 percent FNMAs after taking out 50 basis points for servicing and guaranty fees; and if they are sold forward, no commitment fees are charged. The cash market referred to in each example is one in which delivery takes place immediately.

Going Unhedged

Assume the firm speculates that interest rates will stay the same or rise and leaves the $800,000 in pipeline loans expected to close unhedged.

Interest Rates Stable: If prices stay constant and only 75 percent of the pipeline closes by mid-August, the firm may sell the closed loans for 97:24.

August 17—$750,000 of Pipeline Closes

Sell $750,000			
Delivery Price	97:24		
Weighted Average Cost	97:24		
Gain/Loss	0:00	=	$0

Interest Rates Rise: Prices fall to 95:24 with 85 percent of the pipeline closing by mid-August. The unforseen has happened and the mortgage banker posts a whopping $17,000 loss (.02 × $850,000) when he sells these loans at current market prices.

August 17—$850,000 of Pipeline Closes

Cash Market

Sell $850,000		
Delivery Price	95:24	
Weighted Average Cost	97:24	
Gain/Loss	(2:00)	= ($17,000)

Interest Rates Fall: Prices rise to 99:24 with only 65 percent of the pipeline closing by mid-August. When selling these loans, a total gain of $13,000 is posted (.02 × $650,000).

August 17—$650,000 of Pipeline Closes

Cash Market

Sell $650,000		
Delivery Price	99:24	
Weighted Average Cost	97:24	
Gain/Loss	2:00	= $13,000

An unhedged pipeline can generate either unlimited losses or unlimited gains. Such a strategy is rare and should be consistent with a specific corporate risk/return directive. Most firms attempt to cover the segment of the pipeline expected to close (after fall-out) plus unallocated inventory (closed loans not scheduled for delivery to a specific investor).

Mandatory Coverage

Forward Sale

To avoid interest rate risk, the firm arranges a forward sale of the loans at a price of 97:24. (No commitment fees are charged.) Because only 80 percent of the commitments to borrowers are expected to close, only $800,000 in loans is sold forward.

Since the loans are closed in August and delivered in September, they must be financed for about one month. However, assuming a positive warehouse spread, interest payments on the mortgages may compensate for this additional expense.

Interest Rates Stable: If prices stay constant but only 75 percent of the loans close, the mortgage banker can sell the closed loans for 97:24.

August 17—$750,000 of Pipeline Closes

Cash Market

Buy $50,000

Delivery Price	97:24	
Weighted Average Cost	97:24	
Gain/Loss	0:00	= $0

Forward Sale $800,000

Delivery Price	97:24	
Average Weighted Cost	97:24	
Gain/Loss	0:00	= $0

Interest Rates Climb: Rates have risen so that FNMA 9.5s are trading for 95:24. Even though rates have increased, the mortgage banker is protected by the forward delivery contract; however, it is likely that more than 80 percent of the pipeline will now close, and the additional closings will be sold at a loss.

If 85 percent (instead of the expected 80 percent) of the loans close, the mortgage banker will probably post a $1,000 loss (two percent of $50,000 in extra closings) if he sells those loans at current market rates.

August 17—$850,000 of Pipeline Closes

Cash Market

Sell $50,000

Delivery Price	95:24	
Weighted Average Cost	97:24	
Gain/Loss	(2:00)	= ($1,000)

Forward Sale $800,000

Delivery Price	97:24	
Weighted Average Cost	97:24	
Gain/Loss	0:00	= $0

Total Net Loss	= ($1,000)

Interest Rates Fall: Should prices climb to 99:24, 10 percent loans will be available for 99:24. For this reason, assume only 65 percent of the loans close. As a result, the mortgage banker is $150,000 short in loans for the September delivery. His losses will approximate the point drop in prices times the increase in fallout, or two percent of $150,000 = $3,000.

In order to fill this obligation, the firm can purchase 10 percent FNMA loans or securities in the secondary market and thus "pair off" their position. Since rates have fallen, such loans would be trading at a price greater than the original forward sale, say 99:24. The firm has to purchase $150,000 in 10 percent loans at a price of 99:24 to fill the forward commitment. This represents a two point loss on the $150,000 or $3,000.

August 17—$650,000 of Pipeline Closes

Cash Market

Buy $150,000

Deliver Price	97:24	
Weighted Average Cost	99:24	
Gain/Loss	(2:00)	= ($3,000)

Forward Sale $800,000

Delivery Price	97:24	
Weighted Average Cost	97:24	
Gain/Loss	0:00	= $0

Total Net Loss	= ($3,000)

Compared with an unhedged pipeline, the mandatory forward sale drastically limits losses during falling prices at a minimal cost (in this case forward sale commitment fees were not charged). However, a forward sale also limits gains, and it is vulnerable to miscalculations in fallout, especially when interest rates fall and mortgage prices rise above commitment prices. If prices rise above 97:24 and fallout is higher than expected, losses will be incurred in direct proportion to the unexpected increase in fallout necessitated by purchasing additional loans in the cash market to make up for the lost pipeline.

Futures

Suppose the firm has used futures to protect the $800,000 in pipeline loans it expected to close. Let us say the firm has been keeping an eye on the FNMA 9.5s and T-Bond futures basis spreads and notices it has been fairly constant at about 2:08 over the past two months. It sees that T-Bond September futures are now selling for 95:16. (Basis = cash price of 97:24 – futures price of 95:16 = 2:08.)

The firm calculates that one futures contract of $100,000 equals $80,000 of its 9.5 percent FNMAs. Thus, to cover $800,000 worth, it will need 10 futures contracts, a hedge ratio of 125 percent.

On June 16, the firm shorts (sells) ten September T-Bond contracts totaling $1 million at 95:16.

Interest Rates Stable: If interest rates stay the same, when the loans close in mid-August at 97:24, the firm can sell them for that much at no loss. The futures position can then be liquidated, but at a cost of $2,500 because, between mid-June and mid-August, the futures price started to move closer to that of the underlying security and is now at 95:24. The firm also posts margin interest costs (about $250) and the $45 commission charged on each contract, for a total of $700. The the total loss is then ($2,500) + ($700) = ($3,200).

August 17—$750,000 of Pipeline Closes

Cash Market

Sell $750,000
Delivery Price   97:24

Weighted Average Cost	97:24	
Gain/Loss	0:00	= $0

Futures Market

Sold 10 contracts 6/16	95:16	
Bought 10 contracts 8/17	95:24	
Gain/Loss	(0:08)	= ($2,500)
Transaction Costs		= ($700)
Total Net Loss		= ($3,200)

Interest Rates Climb: If cash market prices fall to 95:24 with $850,000 worth of loans closing, then a loss of .02 times $850,000, or $17,000 would be incurred in the cash market. But in the futures market, prices are now 93:29, down from 95:16. Thus, in the futures market, there would be a $1,593.75 gain per contract (51/32nds change in price times $31.25 for each 1/32 times ten contracts), or a total of $15,937.50. Overall loss: ($17,000) + ($700) + $15,937.50 = ($1,762.510).

August 17—$850,000 of Pipeline Closes

Cash Market

Sell $850,000

Delivery Price	95:24	
Weighted Average Cost	97:24	
Loss	2:00	= ($17,000)

Futures Market

Sold 10 contracts 6/16	95:16	
Bought 10 contracts 8/16	93:29	
Gain 1:19 = $1,593.75 per contract × 10		= $15,937.50
Transaction Costs		= ($700.00)
Total Net Loss		= ($1,762.50)

(Note: Basis has narrowed from 2:08 to 1:27 during the course of the futures position.)

Interest Rates Fall: If cash market prices rise to 99:24 with 65 percent of the pipeline closing, the firm will gain two percent of $650,000, or $13,000 when selling the loans. But when it liquidates its futures position, it loses $1,593.75 per contract, or $15,937.50 total because prices in the futures market have also risen from 95:16 to 97:03; plus an additional $700 in transaction costs. The firm would have a net loss: $13,000 + ($15,937.50) + ($700) = ($3,637.50).

August 17—$650,000 of Pipeline Closes

Cash Market

Sell $650,000
Delivery Price   99:24
Weighted Average Cost   97:24
Gain   2:00   = $13,000

Futures Market

Sold 10 contract 6/16   95:16
Bought 10 contracts 8/17   97:03
Loss 1:19 = ($1,593.75) per contract × 10   = ($15,937.50)

Transaction Costs   = ($700.00)

Total Net Loss   = ($3,637.50)

(Note: Basis has widened from 2:08 to 2:21 over the course of the futures contract.)

In this scenario, selling futures results in a loss even during stable rates. Even though mortgage rates are steady, the futures price over the term of the hedge will move toward the underlying T-Bond or T-Note price.

When mortgage prices fell to 95:24, the decrease in fallout lead to an inefficient hedge because the decrease in the total value of closed mortgages outweighed the gain in the futures position. A narrowing basis also had a negative impact (for explanation see Chapter 2, "Changes in Basis: The Effects").

When prices rose to 99:24, the increase in fallout led to an inefficient hedge that was offset by a widening in basis. Had the basis stayed at 2:08, the loss on the futures position would have been $20,700 instead of $15,937.50 (99:24 [the cash price mid-August] - 97:16 [the futures price mid-August] = 2:08; loss on futures position would then be 97:16 - 95:16 [the futures price mid-June] = 2:00 = $20,000, plus $700 transaction costs).

The futures hedge becomes increasingly less efficient as changes occur in projected fallout and/or basis. For example:

Assume that in the previous scenario the firm had $500,000 worth of closed loans with a weighted average cost of 97:24, which the firm wanted to pool and sell sometime in the future. Under the same conditions, the firm would short six September futures contracts then valued at 95:16.

If prices stay the same, the firm loses $270 in transaction costs and about $100 in margin interest. By mid-August, the value of the futures contract has climbed to 95:24 so the firm loses :08 when they liquidate the position. This translates into a loss of $250 per contract or a total of ($1,500). Thus, total loss if prices stay the same is: ($1,500) + ($270) + ($100) = ($1,870).

If cash market prices fall to 95:24 the firm will lose two percent of $500,000, or $10,000 on the mortgages. But when the firm closes out the futures position, then at 93:29, they make $1,593.75 per contract, times six contracts, or $9,562.50. Total loss: ($10,000) + $9,562.50 + ($270) + ($100) = ($807.50). (Basis narrowed from 2:08 to 1:27.)

If prices rise to 99:24, the firm gains two percent of $500,000, or $10,000 on the mortgages. But when they close out the futures position, then at 97:03, they lose $9,562.50. Total gain: $10,000 + ($9,562.50) + ($270) + ($100) = $67.50 (basis widened from 2:08 to 2:21).

Futures positions losses and gains at various interest rates are marginal in this case mainly because fallout was not a consideration.

Optional Coverage

Standby Commitment

If the firm had decided to use FNMA standby commitments to cover the pipeline, the firm would have acquired a commitment to sell to FNMA $800,000 worth of FNMA 9.5s at 97:24 in September. The fee charge is 1.5 percent, or $12,000.

Interest Rates Stable: If interest rates stayed the same, the firm would lose the fee, $12,000. Although optional commitments are much less liquid than O-T-C options or options on futures, assume the firm is able to sell the standby commitment for half what it costs, and posts a loss of $6,000.

August 17—$750,000 of Pipeline Closes

Cash Market

Sell $750,000		
Delivery Price	97:24	
Weighted Average Cost	97:24	
Gain/Loss	0:00	= $0

Standby Commitment

Bought 6/16	1:16	
Sold 8/17	:24	
Loss	:24	= ($6,000)

Total Net Loss		= ($6,000)

Interest Rates Climb: If prices fell to 95.24 with 85 percent of the loans closing, the firm exercises the option and delivers $800,000 worth of loans at 97.24 and takes a small $1,000 loss on the extra five percent of pipeline that closed. Total loss: ($12,000) cost of standby + ($1,000) = ($13,000).

August 17—$850,000 of Pipeline Closes

Cash Market

Sell $50,000

Delivery Price	95:24	
Weighted Average Cost	97:24	
Loss	2:00	= ($1,000)

Standby Commitment

Delivery $800,000

Delivery Price	97:24	
Weighted Average	97:24	
Gain/Loss	0:00	= $0
Bought 6/16	1:16	
Exercised 8/17		
Fee Loss	1:16	= ($12,000)
Total Net Loss		= ($13,000)

Interest Rates Fall: If prices climb to 99.24 with 65 percent of the loans closing, the firm gains .02 times $650,000, or $13,000, and does not exercise its optional commitment. Total gain: $13,000 + ($12,000) cost of standby = $1,000.

August 17—$650,000 of Pipeline Closes

Cash Market $650,000

Delivery Price	99:24	
Weighted Average Cost	97:24	
Gain	2:00	= $13,000

Standby Commitment

Bought 6/16	1:16	
Not exercised		
Fee Loss	1:16	= ($12,000)
Total Net Gain		= $1,000

It should be noted that although the standby commitment created a floor that limited potential losses, the standby under-performed both the forward sale and futures market in all but times of rising prices because of high up-front fees. As previously mentioned, an important advantage of using options to hedge is that they allow for gains should the market improve. (As you get further away from the strike price, you may consider selling your product into the cash market to protect those gains.)

Over-the-Counter Options

Had the firm decided to use O-T-C options on mortgages, the firm would have bought, from a licensed broker, at-the-money put options on FNMA 10s with an exercise price of 97:24 and a fee of :29 consisting entirely of time value. (O-T-C options on mortgages are quoted in 32nds.) An expiration date of August 31 is specified.

The firm has calculated a delta of 60 percent for these O-T-C options; that is, a one dollar decrease in the value of the underlying FNMA 10 security should cause a 60 cent increase in the value of the put option. To derive a proper hedge ratio, the firm divides the eight contracts to be hedged (each contract is $100,000) by the delta 8/.60 = 13.33, or 13. The firm purchases 13 put options on FNMA 10s for a total up-front fee of $11,781.25.

Interest Rates Stable: If prices remain the same and $750,000 of the pipeline closes, the firm sells the loans that close at no loss. But the options are losing value as the expiration date approaches. The firm paid :29 for them and sells them for :15, thus losing :14 per contract, or ($437.50). Total loss: ($437.50) × 13 = ($5,687.50).

August 17—$750,000 of Pipeline Closes

Cash Market

Sell $750,000	
Delivery Price	97:24
Average Weighted Cost	97:24
Gain/Loss	0:0

O-T-C Options on FNMAs

Bought 13 puts 6/16	:29	
Sold 13 puts 8/17	:15	
Loss :14 = $437.50 per contract × 13		= ($5,687.50)
Total Net Loss		= ($5,687.50)

Interest Rates Rise: Prices fall to 95:24 with 85 percent of the pipeline closing. The firm loses $17,000 on the loans that close (.02 x $850,000).

But the option to sell at 97:24 is worth 2:08 (intrinsic value of 2:00 and time value of :08). The delta has increased to 67 percent because a 2:00 decrease in the value of FNMA 9.5s caused a 1:11 (:43) increase in the value of the put option (43/32 is 67 percent of 64/32). The put options are then sold for a profit of 1:11, or $17,468.75. Net gain: $468.75.

August 17—$850,000 of Pipeline Closes

Cash Market

Sell $850,000		
Delivery Price	95:24	
Weighted Average Cost	97:24	
Loss	2:00	= ($17,000)

O-T-C Options on FNMAs

Bought 13 puts 6/16	:29	
Sold 13 puts 8/17	2:08	
Gain 1:11 = $1,343.75 × 13		= $17,468.75
Total Net Gain		= $468.75

Interest Rates Fall: Prices rise to 99:24, but only 65 percent of the pipeline closes. The firm posts a profit of $13,000 on the $650,000 of pipeline that closes and is sold (.02 × $650,000 = $13,000).

But the options expire worthless and the entire $11,781.25 premium paid for them is lost. Total gain: $13,000 - $11,781.25 = $1,218.75.

August 17—$650,000 of Pipeline Closes

Cash Market

Sell $650,000		
Delivery Price	99:24	
Weighted Average Cost	97:24	
Gain	2:00	= $13,000

O-T-C Options on FNMAs

Bought 13 puts 6/16	:29	
Expired worthless		
Loss :29 = $906.25 per contract × 13		= ($11,781.25)
Total Gain		= $1,218.75

O-T-C options tend to be less costly than standbys because they may be sold more easily to recoup a portion of their up-front fees. The up-front fees paid for O-T-C options are nevertheless significant, and the fees cause them to under perform the forward sale and even futures market during relatively stable interest rate periods. Up-front fees, of course, may be reduced by the purchase of out-of-the-money options, split fee options (see "Option Premiums," Chapter Four), and/or by using a combination of options and forward sales, as will be shown in following sections.

Options on Futures

Under the same conditions, let us assume that the firm decides to use options on futures to cover the $800,000 in pipeline loans they expect to close.

The firm decides to buy at-the-money put options on September T-Note futures with a strike price of 95:16. These options will cost it 50/64 each, consisting entirely of time value and no intrinsic value.

The firm calculates a delta of 65 percent. This means that for every one dollar jump in the price of the futures contracts there will be a sixty-five cent drop in the value of the put option. The firm determines that 10 futures contracts provide a hedge ratio of 80 percent. The number of futures contracts needed to cover the $800,000 in loans is then divided by .65 (10 divided by .65 = 15 options contracts) to achieve the correct coverage with a 65 percent delta.

The firm buys 15 Treasury Note options on September futures that are then selling for 95:16 for a premium of 50/64 each, or a total cost of $11,719.75.

Interest Rates Stable: If prices remain the same until the loans close, the firm would lose $11,618.75 if it allowed the put options to expire worthless. But assume it recoups part of the up-front fees by selling the at-the-money options before they expire for 30/64 each, or a total of $7,031.25. Total loss: ($11,718.75) + $7,031.25 = ($4,687.50).

August 17—$750,000 of Pipeline Closes

Cash Market

Delivery Price	97:24	
Weighted Average Cost	97:24	
Gain/Loss	0:00	= $0

Options on Futures

Bought 15 puts	50/64	
Sold 15 puts	30/64	
Loss 20/64 = $312.50 per contract × 20		= ($4,687.50)
Total Net Loss		= ($4,687.50)

Interest Rates Climb: If prices fall to 95:24 with 85 percent of the loans closing in mid-August, the firm loses two points on the sale of the mortgages, or $17,000. The option to sell at 95:16 when the futures contracts can then be bought for 93:29 is worth 102/64 intrinsic value plus 14/64 in time value. (This means that the delta has stayed at 65 percent because a 102/64 decrease in the value of the futures option resulted in an 66/64 increase in the value of the put option; 66 is about 65 percent of 102). So when the firm sells the put option, they make 116/64 minus 50/64, or 66/64 per contract. This translates into $15,468.75. Total loss: ($17,000) + $15,468.75 = ($1,531.25).

August 17—$850,000 of Pipeline Closes

Cash Market

Delivery Price	95:24	
Weighted Average Cost	97:24	
Loss	2:00	= ($17,000)

Options on Futures

Bought 15 puts 6/16	50/64	
Sold 15 puts 8/17	116/64	
Gain 66/64 = $1,031.25 per contract × 15		= $15,468.75
Total Net Loss		= ($1,531.25)

Interest Rates Fall: If prices rise to 99:24 with 65 percent of the loans closing, the firm would gain .02 times $650,000, or $13,000.

Futures contracts are then bought for 97:10, so the option expires worthless. Total gain: $13,000 + ($11,718.75) = $1,281.25.

August 17—$650,000 of Pipeline Closes

Cash Market

Delivery Price	99:24	
Average Weighted Cost	97:24	
Gain	2:00	= $13,000

Options on Futures

Bought 15 puts 6/16	50/64	
Puts Expire Worthless		
Loss 50/64 = $781.25 per contract × 15		= ($11,718.75)
Total Net Gain		= $1,281.25

When prices fall, options on futures, like O-T-C options on mortgages, lead to fewer losses than standby commitments because they can be sold to recoup a portion of their up-front cost. Unlike forward sales and futures, they will also allow for gains should prices rise.

O-T-C versus Futures Options

In the previous examples, the effects of using options on futures as well as over-the-counter options were shown; both had similar results. In deciding whether to use options on futures or over-the-counter options the following factors should be considered:

- If market direction is difficult to ascertain, choose the option on the underlying instrument with the least amount of basis risk. Over-the-counter options present less basis risk than options on futures because O-T-C options are sold on mortgages that are similar, if not identical, to what most firms are trying to hedge.

- If market direction is more easily identified, the yield spread between mortgages and Treasuries might dictate the best option to use. If the spread is wide, the purchase of a Treasury put will often provide greater value; it is likely that Treasuries will "cheapen" relative to mortgages.

If the spread between Treasuries and mortgages, for example, has reached an annual high of four points, there is a strong chance that this trend will be reversed either by mortgage yields rising or Treasury yields falling. In either case, Treasuries will "cheapen" relative to mortgages.

If the spread is narrower than usual, then a mortgage put might be the better value. The opposite holds for buying a call. When the spread is unusually narrow, consider buying Treasuries. When the spread is unusually wide, consider buying mortgages.

Integrated Strategies

The above scenarios assumed fairly large and totally unexpected swings in interest rates over a two month period to depict the effects of various hedging tools and was used in each case to the exclusion of the others. Hedgers usually have some idea of where interest rates are heading and may use a combination of forwards, futures, and options to take advantage of interest rate expectations, while protecting product from the unexpected. The basic idea behind these strategies is to be over-covered in sell-offs and undercovered in market rallies.

A firm may use a combination of forwards, futures, and out-of-the-money put options in varying amounts, depending on market conditions. This approach requires hedgers to make conjectures on the direction of interest rates in order to put the hedging devices in place. Consider the following example:

Hedging with Blended Coverage

25% Forward Sale, 42% Short Futures, 33% Out-of-the-money Puts

Market conditions used in this next case are different from those in the previous scenarios. The firm is uncertain on June 16th about the future movement of interest rates because they appear to be reasonably stable. The firm has $1.5 million in loans in the pipeline and decides to cover $300,000 of the pipeline expected to close with mandatory coverage and hedge the remaining $900,000 expected to close with a combination of futures and out-of-the-money put options on futures.

Market Action. The lender obtains a 90-day mandatory commitment on June 16th totaling $300,000 and priced at 97:24.

On June 16, it agrees to sell seven September T-Bond contracts totaling $700,000 for 95:16 each. A conversion factor was used to determine that seven contracts would be needed to hedge $500,000 in pipeline mortgages. (The hedge ratio is about 70 percent.)

On June 16, the firm also buys 15 out-of-the-money put option contracts on September T-Note futures totaling $15,000 for 10/64 each, or a total cost of $2,343.75. The strike price is 93:16. The delta in this case is 35 percent, so the number of futures contracts needed to cover the $500,000 in mortgages is divided by .35 to derive the number of options contracts needed: 5/.35 = 14.3 or 15 option contracts.

Interest Rates Stable: If prices stay constant but only 75 percent of the pipeline closes by mid-August, the firm breaks even on the $300,000 forward sale and the other $825,000 in loans that close. Assuming the basis stays the same, the firm closes its futures position at a loss of $1,750 due to the convergence of the futures price and that of the underlying T-Bond then trading at 96:00. It also takes a $440 loss in transaction costs ($45 per contract plus $125 in margin interest). It does not exercise the options on the September futures contracts, then at 95:16, but sells them for half their cost, or 5/64 each. This translates into a net loss of $78.13 per contract, or a total of $1,171.88. Total loss: ($1,750) + ($1,171.88) = ($3,361.88).

August 17—$1,125,000 of Pipeline Closes

Cash Market

Sell $825,000

Delivery Price	97:24	
Average Weighted Cost	97:24	
Gain/Loss	0:00	= $0

Forward Sale $300,000

Delivery Price	97:24	
Weighted Average Cost	97:24	
Gain/Loss	0:00	= $0

Futures

Sold 7 contracts 6/16	95:16	
Bought 7 contracts 8/17	95:24	
Loss	:08	= ($1,750)
Transaction Costs		= ($440)

Options on Futures

Bought 15 puts 6/16	10/64	
Sold 15 puts 8/17	05/64	
Loss 05/64 = $78.13 per contract × 15		= ($1,171.88)
Total Net Loss		= ($3,361.88)

Interest Rates Climb: If prices fall slightly to 97:16 with 90 percent of the loans closing, the firm breaks even on the $300,000 in loans sold forward, but the other $900,000 in closings incur a $2,250 loss at current market rates (:08 × $900,000).

In mid-August, September futures are at 95:10. The firm agrees to sell seven such contracts at 95:16, so the firm makes a profit of $187.50 per contract (6 × $31.25) or a total of $1,312.50 minus $440 in transaction costs, or a net gain of $872.50.

The out-of-the-money put options on September futures are at 14/64 in mid-August, so they are sold for a profit of 4/64, or $62.50 per contract. Total gain is 15 × $62.50, or $937.50.

Total loss: ($2,250) + $1,312.50 + ($440) + $937.50 = ($440).

August 17—$1,200,000 of Pipeline Closes

Cash Market

Sell $900,000

Delivery Price	97:16	
Average Weighted Cost	97:24	
Loss	:08	= ($2,250)

Forward Sale $300,000

Delivery Price	97:24	
Average Weighted Cost	97:24	
Gain/Loss	0:00	

Futures

Sold 7 contracts 6/16	95:16	
Bought 7 contracts 8/17	95:10	
Gain: 06 = $187.50 per contract × 7		= $1,312.50
Transaction Costs		= ($440)

Options on Futures

Bought 10 puts 6/16	10/64	
Sold 10 puts 8/17	14/64	
Gain 04/64 = $62.50 per contract × 15		= $937.50
Total Net Loss		= ($440)

Interest Rates Fall: If prices rise slightly to 98:00 with 70 percent of the loans closing, the firm still breaks even on the $300,000 in loans sold forward. On the other $750,000 that close by mid-August, it posts a profit of $1,875 at current market rates (:08 × $750,000).

In mid-August, September futures are at 95:22 and the firm has agreed to sell seven such contracts for 95:16. It posts a loss of :06 per contract, or a total of $1,312.50 ($186.50 × seven contracts).

Total loss on the futures position is then $1,312.50 + $440 in transaction costs, or $1,752.50.

The out-of-the-money put options on September futures are at 06/64 in mid-August, so they are sold at a loss of 4/64 per contract, or a total of $937.50 ($62.50 × 15 contracts).

Total loss: $1,875 + ($1,312.50) + ($440) + ($937.50) = ($815).

August 17—$1,050,000 of Pipeline Closes

Cash Market

Sell $750,000

Delivery Price	98:00	
Weighted Average Cost	97:24	
Gain	:08	= $1,875

Forward Sale $300,000

Delivery Price	97:24	
Weighted Average Cost	97:24	
Gain/Loss	0:0	= $0

Futures

Sold 7 contracts 6/16	95:16	
Bought 7 contracts 8/17	95:22	
Loss: 06 = $187.50 per contract × 7		= ($1,312.50)
Transaction Costs		= ($440)

Options on Futures

Bought 10 puts 6/16	10/64	
Sold 10 puts 8/17	06/64	
Loss 04/64 = $62.50 per contract × 15		= ($937.50)

Total Net Loss	= ($815)

In the above example, changes in interest rates and fallout were quite small, so the use of futures in a combination strategy worked well. But in volatile markets where uncertainty about interest rates and fallout prevail, the firm is probably better off avoiding the futures market and using combinations of options and forward sales. In volatile markets, selling futures becomes vulnerable to changes in fallout and/or basis that may lead to poten-tially unlimited losses. Use of options, however, limits losses to the option premium. If mortgage prices drop below the strike price of the put, the firm can always exercise the put, thereby neutralizing some of the loss on the cash position.

In using a combination of forward sales and options, the hedger sells forward that part of the pipeline that he is positive will close. By doing so, the number of options contracts needed and up-front fees are thus reduced.

In the following scenarios interest rates are assumed to fluc-tuate by plus or minus two points and fallout will vary according-ly. As in the first section, the firm in mid-June has $1 million in 10 percent loans in the pipeline which they expect to sell as 9.5 per-cent FNMA securities. The pipeline loan commitments are for 60 days and it expects 80 percent of the pipeline loans to close by mid-August.

40% Forward Sale, 40% At-the-Money Puts

A combination of at-the-money put options and a forward sale can out-perform the pure at-the-money put option hedge during rising or stable interest rates because the put option fee in each of the pure option hedges exceeds the opportunity cost of the forward sale. During falling rates, however, an at-the-money put option strategy provides a more profitable hedge because the op-tion fee is less than the opportunity cost of the forward sale.

Desired Strategy. The lender is fairly certain that interest rates in the next two months will remain stable or else rise. He decides to cover 40 percent of the pipeline ($400,000 in loans) expected to close with mandatory commitments; the remaining 40 percent ex-pected to close is hedged with at-the-money puts.

Market Action. On June 16, the firm obtains a 90-day forward commitment for $400,000 of loans. The commitment is priced at 97:24.

On June 16, the lender buys eight at-the-money put option contracts (delta is 65 percent) on September T-Note futures. The strike price is 95:16 and the premium is 50/64, or $781.25 per con-tract. The total up-front fee paid for the options is $6,250.

Interest Rates Stable: If prices stay the same and $750,000 worth of pipeline loans close by mid-August, the firm breaks even on the mandatory sale arranged in June as well as the $350,000 it sells into the current market.

But because interest rates are steady, the at-the-money put options on September futures are losing value as their expiration date approaches. The eight puts bought in June at 50/64 can be sold in mid-August for only 25/64, resulting in a 25/64 loss for each. Dollar loss per contract is $390.63 (25 × $15.625), or a total of $3,125.04 (8 × $390.63).

Total loss: ($3,125.04).

August 17—$750,000 of Pipeline Closes

Cash Market

Sell $350,000
Delivery Price   97:24
Weighted Average Cost   97:24
Gain/Loss   0:0 = $0

Forward Sale $400,000

Delivery Price   97:24
Weighted Average Cost   97:24
Gain/Loss   0:0 = $0

Options on Futures

Bought 8 puts 6/16   50/64
Sold 8 puts 8/17   25/64
Loss 25/64 = $390.63 per contract × 8   = ($3,125.04)

Total Net Loss   = ($3,125.04)

Interest Rates Rise: Prices fall to 95:24 with 85 percent of the pipeline closing by mid-August. The firm breaks even on the mandatory sale arranged in June, but loses $9,000 (2.0 × $450,000) on the other $450,000 of loans that close by mid-August.

The options transaction makes up most of those losses because September futures in mid-August can be bought for 93:29, and the firm has the option to sell them for 95:16. That option is worth 102/64 in intrinsic value plus 14/64 in time value, or a total of 116/64; they were purchased for 50/64. So by selling the eight at-the-money puts in August, the firm makes $1,031.25 per put (116/24 - 50/64 = 66/64; 66/64 × $15.625 per 1/64), or a total of $8,250.

Total loss: ($9,000) + $8,250   = ($750.00).

August 17—$850,000 of Pipeline Closes

Cash Market

Sell $450,000			
Delivery Price	95:24		
Average Weighted Cost	97:24		
Loss	2:00	= ($9,000)	

Forward Sale	$400,000	
Delivery Price	97:24	
Average Weighted Cost	97:24	
Gain/Loss	0:0	

Options on Futures

Bought 8 contracts 6/16	50/64	
Sold 8 contracts 8/17	116/64	
Gain 66/64 = $1,031.25 per contract × 8		= $8,250

Total Net Loss	= ($750)

Interest Rates Fall: Prices climb to 99:24 with only 65 percent ($650,000 in loans) of the pipeline closing. The firm breaks even on the mandatory sale. The remaining $250,000 in loans that closes are sold at a two point gain, or $5,000.

But the firm loses on the options transaction. September futures are being bought for 97:03 and the firm has an option to sell them at 95:16. That option is no longer traded, and it expires worthless. This means that the entire $6,250 up-front fee paid for the option is lost.

Total loss: $5,000 + ($6,250)   = ($1,250).

August 17—$650,000 of Pipeline Closes

Cash Market

Sell $250,000
Delivery Price	99:24	
Average Weighted Cost	97:24	
Gain	2:00	= $5,000

Forward Sale	$400,000	
Delivery Price	97:24	
Average Weighted Cost	97:24	
Gain/Loss	0:0	= $0

Options on Futures

Bought 8 puts 6/16	50/64	
Puts Expire Worthless		
Loss 50/64 = $781.25 per contract × 8		= ($6,250)
Total loss		= ($1,250)

Options Hedging with Multiple Strike Prices

40% Forward, 20% Out-of-the-Money, 20% At-the-Money Puts

By using a specific combination of multiple strike prices in constructing a put option hedge, a firm can attain close to breakeven results over a wide spectrum of price moves.

Desired Strategy. The lender is uncertain about which way interest rates will head. To protect against a downturn in the market, he sells forward 40 percent ($400,000 in loans) of the pipeline expected to close and buys out-of-the-money and at-the-money put options on remaining 40 percent expected to close.

Market Action. On June 16, the firm sells forward $400,000 in loans priced at 97:24 through a 90-day commitment.

On June 16, the firm buys eight out-of-the-money put option contracts on September futures then at 95:16. Strike price is 94:24 and the premium is 15/64. The delta for these options is 35 percent. The lender also buys four at-the-money puts on September futures. The strike price is 97:00 and the premium is 50/64. Delta for these options is 65 percent.

% of Pipeline

Covered by Options	Strike Price	Fee	Cost per Contract
20 percent	94:24	15/64	$234.38
$200,000 in loans	(Out-of-the-$)		
20 percent	95:16	50/64	$781.25
$200,000 in loans	(At-the-$)		

Interest Rates Stable: Prices stay the same and 75 percent of the pipeline closes. The firm breaks even on the $400,000 in loans sold forward as well as the $350,000 that close in August and are sold at current market prices.

But because interest rates are stable, the value of the put options is decreasing as their expiration date approaches. The out-of-the-money puts bought for a premium of 15/64 each can be sold in mid-August for 08/64. Loss is 7/64 (7 × 15.625 × 8) or $875. The at-the-money puts bought for 50/64 are sold for only 25/64. Loss is 25/64 (25 × 15.625 × 4 contracts) = ($1,562.50).

Total loss: ($875) + ($1,562.50)   = ($2,437.50).

August 17—$750,000 of Pipeline Closes

Cash Market

Sell $350,000
Delivery Price   97:24
Average Weighted Cost   97:24
Gain/Loss   0:0   = $0

Forward Sale $400,000

Delivery Price   97:24
Average Weighted Cost   97:24
Gain/Loss   0:0   = $0

Options on Futures

Bought 8 puts 6/16	15/64
Sold 8 puts 8/17	08/64
Loss 07/64 = $109.38 per contract × 8	= ($875)

Bought 4 puts 6/16	50/64
Sold 4 puts 8/17	25/64
Loss 25/64 = $390.63 per contract × 4	= ($1,562.50)
Total net loss	= ($2,437.50)

Interest Rates Rise: Prices fall to 95:24 with 85 percent ($850,000 in loans) of the pipeline closing. The firm breaks even on the forward sale, but on the cash market sale of the other $450,000 in loans that close, loses $9,000 (2.0 × $450,000).

September futures in mid-August can be bought for 93:29, so the out-of-the-money put is worth 54/64 in intrinsic value plus 06/64 in time value, or a total of 60/64. (Notice that the delta in this case has moved from 35 percent to 44 percent; a 102/64 drop in the price of the futures contract led to a 45/64 rise in the options price.) Since the out-of-the-money puts were bought for 15/64 and sold for 60/64, a 45/64 profit is posted. In dollar terms this means a gain of $4,625 (45 × 15.625 × eight contracts).

In mid-August, the at-the-money-put option is worth 102/64 in intrinsic value plus 14/64 in time value, or a total of 116/64. Since these puts were bought for 50/64 and sold for 116/64, a 66/64 profit is posted. This means a gain of 66/64 or $4,125 (66 × 15.625 × four contracts).

Total gain: ($9,000) + $5,625 + $4,125 = $750.

August 17—$850,000 of Pipeline Closes

Cash Market

Sell $450,000		
Delivery Price	95:24	
Average Weighted Cost	97:24	
Loss	2:00	= ($9,000)

Forward Sale $400,000

Delivery Price	97:24	
Average Weighted Cost	97:24	
Gain/Loss	0:0	= $0

Options on Futures

Bought 8 puts 6/16	15/64	
Sold 8 puts 8/17	60/64	
Gain 45/64 = $703.13 per contract × 8		= $5,625

Bought 4 puts 6/16	50/64	
Sold 4 puts 8/17	116/64	
Gain 66/64 = $1,031.25 per contract × 4		= $4,125

Total Net Gain	= $750

Interest Rates Fall: Prices rise to 99:24 with only 65 percent of the pipeline closing. A breakeven on the forward sale is attained and the remaining $250,000 in loans that close are sold in the cash market for a two point gain or $5,000 (2.0 × $250,000).

But money is lost on the options position. September futures can be bought for 97:03 in mid-August, so the eight out-of-the-money options expire worthless, and the $1,875 up-front fee paid to acquire the options is lost.

The at-the-money put options that were purchased are now out-of-the-money, and they also expire worthless for a loss of $3,125. The total loss on the combined options position is: ($1,875) + ($3,125) = ($5,000).

Thus, if prices rise by two points, the firm breaks even: $5,000 + ($1,875) + ($3,125) = $0.

August 17—$650,000 of Pipeline Closes

Cash Market

Sell $250,000

Delivery Price	99:24	
Weighted Average Cost	97:24	
Gain	2:00	= $5,000

Forward Sale $400,000

Delivery Price	97:24
Weighted Average Cost	97:24
Gain/Loss	0:0

Options on Futures

Bought 8 puts 6/16	15/64	
Expired worthless		
Loss 15/64 = $234.38 per contract × 8		= ($1,875)

Bought 4 puts 6/16	50/64	
Expire worthless		
Loss 50/64 = $781.25 per contract × 4		= ($3,125)
Total Net Gain/loss		= $0

Notice that this particular combination of strike prices (out-of-the-money and at-the-money) results in nearly balanced results should rates rise by two points ($750 gain) or fall by two points ($0.00 gain/loss). It results also in fewer losses than the previous two options strategies should interest rates remain stable. Had the firm felt strongly that rates were going to rise, it could have biased the hedge for a downturn in the market by using a preponderance of in-the-money puts.

Combination Strategies with Options

Compound options, synthetic puts, and spreads and straddles are advanced options strategies that may be used to fine tune a hedge. (A description of these options strategies is in Chapter III under "Option Combos.") It should be noted at the outset that such options positions are much more complex than the purchase of put options detailed thus far. This is not to suggest that these types of strategies should not be considered. But, before undertaking any of them, a firm must have a good understanding of options and consult with an experienced and knowledgeable options broker on the risks and potential rewards of such strategies under various market conditions.

Hedging with Compound Options/Split Fee Options

40% Forward, 20% Put Options, 20% Compound Puts

Desired Strategy. The firm wants to protect the pipeline from rising rates using options, but also wants to save on up-front option fees. The firm decides to use compound options for part of the pipeline.

Compound options and split fee options, essentially options on options, are sold *only* on over-the-counter markets. To buy one compound option, the purchaser pays a small fee, called the first fee or initial fee and, subsequently, a decision must be made whether or not to buy the underlying option. The date for this decision is called first expiration and the fee that would be paid to buy the underlying option is called the second fee or first strike. The day the underlying option expires is called the second expiration and its price, the second strike.

A straight put option will have a higher initial fee than the compound or split fee put, but will cost less in total than the compound options if the second fee is paid. For this reason, these options should probably only be used when a firm is fairly certain that prices will rise (and only the initial fee of the option is paid), but still wants to cover against a downturn in the market.

Market Action. On June 16, $400,000 in FNMA 10s are sold forward at 97:24 for a 90-day delivery.

On June 16, three split fee put options on FNMAs 10s with a first expiration in 60 days, second expiration in 90 days and an underlying strike price of 97:24 are bought for :14 each. (Over-the counter option premiums are quoted in 32nds.)

On June 16, three at-the-money put options are bought on FNMA 10s, expiration in 90 days. The strike price is 97:24 and the premium is :29. Delta is 60 percent.

Option Premiums

	First Fee	Second Fee
Split Fee Option	0:14	0:24
Straight Put	0:29	0:00

Interest Rates Stable: Prices stay the same with 75 percent of pipeline closing. The firm breaks even on the $400,000 forward sale as well on the other $350,000 in loans that close and are sold at current market prices.

There is no need to exercise the compound options so they expire worthless and the $1,312.50 up-front fee paid for them (14 × $31.25 × three contracts) is lost.

The puts on FNMAs are losing value as their expiration date nears and are sold in mid-August for :15, resulting in a :14 loss on each. This translates into a $1,312.50 loss (14 × $31.25 × three contracts).

Total loss: ($1,312.50) + ($1,312.50) = ($2,625).

August 18—$750,000 of Pipeline Closes

Cash Market

Sell $350,000

Delivery Price	97:24	
Average Weighted Cost	97:24	
Gain/Loss	0:0	= $0

Forward Sale $400,000

Delivery Price	97:24	
Average Weighted Cost	97:24	
Gain/Loss	0:0	= $0

Compound Options

Bought 3 puts 6/16	:14	
Expired worthless		
Loss :14 = $437.50 per contract × 3		= ($1,312.50)

Standard O-T-C Options

Bought 3 puts 6/16	:29	
Sold 3 puts 8/17	:15	
Loss :14 = $437.50 per contract × 3		= ($1,312.50)

Total Net Loss	= ($2,625)

Interest Rates Rise: Prices fall to 95:24 with 85 percent of the loans closing. A breakeven is attained on the forward sale but a $9,000 loss (2.0 × $450,000) is posted on the remaining $450,000 in loans that close.

In early August before the compound option expires, the firm notices that FNMA prices were dropping so they exercised the three compound options and bought three options for :24 each to sell FNMA 10s at 97:24 by the end of August. In mid-August, after 85 percent of the pipeline closed, the firm sells the options. Since FNMAs in mid-August can be bought for about 95:24, the option to sell for 97:24 is worth 2:00 in intrinsic value plus :08 in time value. For each compound option the gain is 2:08 less :14 paid for the first fee plus :24 paid for the second fee, or a net gain of 1:02 (:34). This translates into $1,062.50 per contract (34 × $31.25), or a total of $3,187.50.

In mid-August, the three regular O-T-C options with strikes of 97:24 are also worth 2:00 in intrinsic value and :08 in time value. Since they were bought for :29 each, there is a net 1:11 gain on their sale, or a total of $4,031.25.

Total loss: ($9,000) + $3,187.50 + $4,031.25 = ($1,781.25).

August 17—$850,000 of Pipeline Closes

Cash Market
Sell $450,000

Delivery Price	95:24	
Weighted Average Cost	97:24	
Loss	2:00	= ($9,000)

Forward Sale $400,000

Delivery Price	97:24	
Weighted Average Cost	97:24	
Gain/Loss	0:0	= $0

Compound Options

Bought 3 puts 6/16	:14	
Exercised 3 puts		
Bought 2 puts 8/1	:24	
Sold 2 puts 8/17	2:08	
Gain 1:02 = $1,062.50 per contract × 3		= $3187.50

Standard OTC Options

Bought 3 puts 6/16	:29	
Sold 3 puts 8/17	2:08	
Gain 1:11 = $1,343.75 per contract × 3		= $4031.25
Total Net Loss		= ($1,781.25)

Interest Rates Fall: Prices rise to 99:24 with 65 percent of the pipeline closing. The firm breaks even on the $400,000 in loans sold forward in June and makes $5,000 (2.0 × $250,000) on the cash market sale of the other $250,000 in loans that close by mid-August.

In early August when the compound option was due to expire, the firm noticed that FNMA prices were rising and did not exercise the option, thereby posting a :14 loss of $1,312.50 (14 × $31.25 × three contracts) on the three compound options bought in June.

By mid-August FNMA 9.5s can be bought for about 99:24, so the option to sell them at 97:24 expires worthless. The firm loses the :29 premium on each of the three regular O-T-C options, or a total $2,718.75 (29 × $31.25 × three contracts).

Total gain: $5,000 + ($1,312.50) + ($2,718.75) = $968.75.

August 17—$650,000 of Pipeline Closes

Cash Market

Sell $250,000

Delivery Price	99:24	
Weighted Average Cost	97:24	
Gain	2:00	= $5,000

Forward Sales $400,000

Delivery Price	97:24	
Weighted Average Cost	97:24	
Gain/Loss	0:0	= $0

Compound Options

Bought 3 puts 6/16	:14	
Expired worthless		
Loss :14 = $437.50 per contract × 3		= ($1,312.50)

Standard O-T-C Options

Bought 3 puts 6/16	:29
Expired worthless	
Loss :29 = $906.25 each × 3	= ($2,718.75)
Total Net Gain	= $968.75

The combination of a forward sale and compound option performs better in rising markets and worse in falling markets than either of the other options strategies. This is because in a falling market, the compound option is in-the-money at the first expiration date and is exercised; the second fee is greater than the fee for the straight option. In a rising market, the second fee is not incurred and the first fee for the compound option is less than the fee for the straight option. For this reason, the compound option is said to be a more "bullish" security (that is, performs better during rising mortgage prices) than the regular put option.

Hedging with Synthetic Puts

80% Forward, 80% Out-of-the-Money Calls

Desired Strategy. Assume that interest rates have been climbing for quite a while and reliable sources indicate that they have now peaked. A firm may create a synthetic put by selling forward 80 percent ($800,000) of the pipeline expected to close and buying out-of-the-money call options on the same 80 percent. The forward sale protects the pipeline during rising interest rates. On the other hand, if the market rallies, the calls prevent fallout related losses on the short position. (A synthetic call would be on mandatory commitments and put options on 80 percent of the pipeline—essentially the option strategy described in the first section of this chapter.)

Market Action. On June 16, the firm obtains a 90-day mandatory commitment totaling $800,000 and priced at 97:24.

On June 16, it also buys 23 out-of-the-money call option contracts on FNMA 9.5s then priced at 97:24. The strike price is 99:24 and the premium is :10. Delta is 35 percent.

Interest Rates Stable: Prices stay the same with 75 percent of the pipeline closing. The firm breaks even on the $800,000 in loans sold forward in mid-June.

But by mid-August the eight 23 options have lost half their value and are sold for :05. The loss is 5 × $31.25 × 23, or $3,593.75.

Total loss if prices remain the same is ($3,593.75).

August 17—$750,000 of Pipeline Closes

Cash Market

Buy $50,000
Delivery Price	97:24
Weighted Average Cost	97:24
Gain/Loss	0:0

Forward Sale $800,000

Delivery Price	97:24
Average Weighted Cost	97:24
Gain/Loss	0:0

O-T-C Options on FNMAs

Bought 23 calls 6/16	:10	
Sold 23 calls 8/17	:05	
Loss :05 = $156.25 per contract × 23		= ($3,593.75)
Total Net Loss		= ($3,593.75)

Interest Rates Rise: Prices fall to 95:24 with 85 percent of the pipeline closing. The firm breaks even on the $800,000 forward sale. The extra $50,000 in loans that close by mid-August result in a $1,000 loss (2.0 × $50,000).

As mortgage prices start to fall, the firm notices that the options contracts are losing value. The firm sells them as soon as interest rates start to rise because the pipeline will still be protected by the forward sale. So assume at the end of June the firm sells the call options for :07, taking a :03 loss on each. This translates into a loss of $2,156.25 (3 × $31.25 × 23 contracts).

Total loss: ($1,000) + ($2,156.25) = ($3,156.25).

August 17—$850,000 of Pipeline Closes

Cash Market

Sell $50,000

Delivery Price	95:24	
Weighted Average Cost	97:24	
Loss	2:00	= ($1,000)

Forward Sale $800,000

Delivery Price	97:24	
Weighted Average Cost	97:24	
Gain/Loss	0:0	

Options on FNMA 9.5s

Bought 23 calls 6/16	:10	
Sold 23 calls 6/30	:07	
Loss :03 = $93.75 per contract × 23		= ($2,156.25)
Total Net Loss		= ($3,156.25)

Interest Rates Fall: Prices rise to 99:24 with 65 percent of the pipeline closing. The firm has sold forward $800,000 in loans but only $650,000 close. The firm must pay an extra two points to buy the required $150,000 in loans needed to fill the commitment. In doing so they post a $3,000 loss (2.0 × $150,000).

In mid-August, the call options to buy FNMA 9.5s for 99:24 have a value of :16. Gain on the sale of the 23 FNMA calls is then :16 or a total of $11,500 (16 × $31.25 × 23 contracts).

Total gain: ($3,000) + $11,5000 = $8,500.

August 17—$650,000 of Pipeline Closes

Cash Market

Buy $150,000

Delivery Price	97:24	
Weighted Average Cost	99:24	
Loss	2:00	= ($3,000)

Forward Sale $800,000
Delivery Price   97:24
Weighted Average Cost   97:24
Gain/Loss   0:0

O-T-C Options on FNMAs

Bought 23 calls 6/16   :10
Sold 23 calls 8/17   :26
Gain :16 = $500 per contract × 23   = $11,500

Total Net Gain   = $8,500

While the synthetic put is more costly in this example than the synthetic call during rising interest rates, it results in much higher profits should interest rates fall.

Hedging with Option Spreads

40% Forward, 40% Call Option Spread

Desired Strategy. The firm thinks that interest rates will remain neutral or else fall and decides to construct a call option spread. The most basic put and call option spreads are created by simultaneously buying and selling puts or calls with different strike prices.

Spreads are more complicated and risky to use than regular options and should be used sparingly. When using spreads the firm must consider: (1) the difficulty that may be involved in attempting to simultaneously execute two or more buy or sell orders at the desired prices; (2) the possibility that a loss could be posted on both options transactions; and (3) the increased exposure that would result from the exercise and liquidation of one side of the trade while the other side of the trade remains outstanding.

One of the main advantages of spreads is that they allow the firm to post gains in a neutral market. The drawback is that the lender loses the entire amount of the call spread (the difference between the profits made when selling a call and losses posted from buying the call) should interest rates rise and the entire amount of the put spread should interest rates fall.

Resistance to time value decay is a main attraction of spreads. Only during the last four to six weeks before expiration are options spreads strongly affected by the passage of time. At this time, a decision should be made to either hold onto an in-the-money spread which is bound to appreciate or to liquidate an out-of-the-money spread bound to depreciate.

Let us consider the price behavior through time of two different call spreads on futures versus a naked call, assuming no change in the underlying futures prices. Notice the severe time value decay of the call versus that of the spreads.

Market Action. On June 16, the firm sells forward $400,000 in loans at 97:24 for delivery in three months.

On June 16, the firm sells 11 at-the-money call option contracts on FNMA 10s then at 97:24. A premium of :29 per contract is earned, or a total of $9,968.75 ($906.25 × 11 contracts).

On June 16, the firm buys 11 out-of-the-money call option contracts on FNMA 10s. The strike price is 99:24. A premium of :08 per contract is paid, or a total of $2,750 ($250 × 11 contracts).

Interest Rates Stable. Prices stay the same, and 75 percent of the pipeline closes. The firm breaks even on the $400,000 forward sale and on the cash market sale of the other $350,000 in loans that close by mid-August.

In mid-August the out-of-the-money put options are not trading and they expire worthless. This translates into a loss of $2,750 —the entire premium.

Since prices in general are stable through August, the call options to buy FNMA 10s at 97:24 that were sold in June are not exercised. But in order to protect itself, the firm cancelled its writing position by buying 11 call options on FNMA 10s at the end of June for :20 per contract or a total cost of $6,875.00.

Total Gain: $9,968.75 + ($2,750) + ($6,875) = $343.75.

August 17—$750,000 of Pipeline Closes

Cash Market

Sell $350,000

Delivery Price	97:24
Weighted Average Cost	97:24
Gain/Loss	0:0

Forward Sale $400,000

Delivery Price	97:24	
Weighted Average Cost	97:24	
Gain/Loss	0:0	= $0

O-T-C Options on FNMAs

Bought 11 calls 6/16   :08
Expire worthless
Loss :08 = $250 per contract × 11   = ($2,750)
Sold 11 calls 6/16 :29 = $906.25 per contract × 11
                                             = $9,968.75
Bought 11 calls 6/30 :20 = $625 per contract × 11
                                             = ($6,875.00)
Gain :09 = $281.25 per contract × 11   = $3,093.65

Total Net Gain   = $343.75

Interest Rates Rise. Prices fall to 95:24 with 85 percent of the pipeline closing. The firm breaks even on the $400,000 forward sale but posts a $9,000 loss (2.0 × $450,000) on the cash market sale of the other $450,000 in loans that close.

By mid-August, the call option to buy FNMA 9.5s at 99:24 are not trading and expire worthless. The loss is $2,750.

Because FNMA 9.5s continue selling for 95:24 through August, the call option to buy at 97:24 that the firm sold in June expires worthless. The firm posts a gain of $9,968.75.

Total loss: ($9,000) + ($2,750) + $9,968.75 = ($1,781.25).

August 17—$850,000 of Pipeline Closes

Cash Market

Sell $450,000

Delivery Price	95:24	
Average Weighted Cost	97:24	
Loss	2:00	= ($9,000)

Forward Sale $400,000

Delivery Price	97:24	
Average Weighted Cost	97:24	
Gain/Loss	0:0	= $0

O-T-C Options on FNMAs

Bought 11 calls 6/16	:08	
Expire worthless		
Loss :08 = ($250) per contract × 11		= ($2,750.00)

Sold 11 calls 6/16	:29	
Not exercised		
Gain :29 = $906.25 per contract × 11		= $9,968.75

Total Net Loss		= ($1,781.25)

Interest Rates Fall. Prices rise to 99:24 with 65 percent of the pipeline closing. A breakeven is attained on the $400,000 forward sale and the other $250,000 in loans that close show a gain of $5,000 (.02 × $250,000).

In mid-August, options to buy FNMA 10s at 99:24 have a time value of :16 and are sold for a profit of :08 each, or a total gain of $2,750.

Because futures prices are rising there is a good chance the call option sold in June will be exercised. The firm offsets the position in late June by buying eleven call options with a strike price of 97:24 on FNMA 10s. Since FNMA 10s were then selling 98:08, the firm paid a premium of 1:12 for each call (:16 intrinsic value and :28 time value). This translates into a total cost of :44 per contract or a total of $15,125 (44 × $31.25 × eleven contracts). Net loss on call writing is $15,125 minus the $9,968.75 profit from selling the calls, or $5,156.25.

Total gain is: $5,000 + $2,750 + $9,968.75 + ($15,125) = $2,593.75.

August 17—$650,000 of Pipeline Closes

Cash Market

Sell $250,000		
Delivery Price	99:24	
Weighted Average Cost	97:24	
Gain	2:00	= $5,000

Forward Sale $400,000		
Delivery Price	97:24	
Weighted Average Cost	97:24	
Gain/Loss	0:0	= $0

O-T-C Options on FNMAs

Bought 11 calls 6/16	:08	
Sold 11 calls 8/17	:16	
Gain :08 = $250 per contract × 11		= $2,750
Sold 11 calls 6/16	:29	
Bought 11 calls 6/30	1:12	
Loss :15 = $468.75 per contract × 11		= ($5,156.25)
Total Net Gain		= $2,593.75

The call option spread is the only option strategy that results in gains during stable interest rates due to the premium income from writing calls. One of the main dangers of spreads, however, is the unlimited losses that may result from selling options. In this case, the firm was able to recoup losses on the options position during falling interest rates through cash market gains.

5

Marketing
Management

There are substantial financial risks involved in hedging, pricing, and other marketing activities associated with the time frame between loan origination and closing. Management and control of the marketing department is key to the successful operation of a mortgage banking business. Effective management of interest rate risk entails the coordination of three primary considerations—marketing strategy, marketing information, and marketing execution. In a company with a large volume of loan activity, marketing execution, the actual buying and selling of loans and hedge positions, can be an extremely dynamic process whereby decisions involving millions of dollars are made daily. To control this activity effectively, senior management must clearly define its marketing strategy and related policy parameters, plus establish control mechanisms that will ensure that the execution of trades is consistent with the firm's strategies and policies.

How Much Risk is Appropriate?

It is the responsibility of the corporation through its board of directors or senior management to determine the level of risk that is acceptable in order to achieve overall corporate goals: they license risk-taking. The risk manager ensures that this level of risk is not exceeded.

Therefore, how does the corporation determine how much risk is appropriate? First, management must decide how much money the company is willing to lose in marketing. If the answer is that it does not want to lose or cannot afford to lose much money, then its appetite for risk is extremely low and its marketing strategies should be conservative. On the other hand, if it is willing to lose and can afford to lose a substantial sum, then its taste for risk is high and its marketing strategies can be extremely aggressive. Varying degrees of risk between both ends of this spectrum can also be utilized.

Second, management must translate its willingness to assume risk into terms that are completely understood by the risk manager. Generally, this means giving the manager a budgeted figure for marketing profits and losses. The conservative strategy will target a breakeven on loan sales, while the aggressive strategy will aim for a gain. Management must acknowledge that opportunities for marketing profits create commensurate opportunities for marketing losses. It is crucial that senior management authorize a dollar value risk limit.

Defining Pricing Policies

Creation of, and adherence to, corporate pricing policies is critical to effective interaction between marketing, production, and servicing. This policy must consider marketing risk and should be reviewed periodically to ensure that it reflects current market conditions and corporate sentiment.

A company must decide what types of loans to produce and service. Owner-occupied, investor, condominiums, townhouses, manufactured housing, bi-weekly payments, and geographic limitations are a few of the types of mortgage situations that need to be identified. Lack of product can put a company at a market disadvantage, but too many products can cripple efficiency. For this reason, the number of offerings that can be managed effectively by the marketing, operations, and production staffs should not be exceeded.

Next, the rate/price guarantee policy needs to be defined: 60-, 45-, 30-, 15-, five-, or two-day quotes are the most common. The longer the commitment period, the higher the risk due to greater fallout potential. In general, there is a tendency to price the shorter-term loan guarantees more aggressively because they can be delivered into earlier commitments, and they have less fallout. Some companies only offer five- or ten-day guarantees, while others give ones with 90, 60, 45, or 30 days. The ability to approximate fallout for any period is essential when offering long-term guarantees; and guarantee periods that do not reasonably ensure that the loan can be closed before expiration should not be allowed. Management must also decide if guarantees are to be in writing, and if so, provide the language that details the terms. If a loan officer can quote a price that is better or worse than the "corporate" price, the conditions under which this can be done and the limits should be set forth in writing.

How often prices will be made available—daily, weekly, more than once a day—and for what length of time should also be determined. Again, this policy must be set in the context of the risk involved. Prices that are set on a weekly basis are extremely risky, while those that are set hourly or daily have reduced risk. The hours that prices can be obtained are important also. If the company offers a daily price, will that price be good for 24 hours or four hours? The longer the price is available, the greater the risk will be in a volatile market.

The people authorized to change prices need to be defined. Are underages and overages allowed? Are there pricing limits, and must the pricing discretion be approved? Once prices are established, will they be the same corporate-wide, or will there be regional or branch specific pricing?

Price can be used effectively to encourage or discourage certain types of business. If higher balance conventional loans are desired, either lower discounts or a credit to the loan officer can induce this business. Higher discounts are appearing on VA loans due to the cost associated with VA no bids.

Is the company trying to establish a presence in a new market? More aggressive prices may be tolerated to get loan officers in the doors of Realtor offices. Is production slack? More aggressive prices may be a stimulant. Perhaps there are processing delays due to too many loans in the system, and pricing can be made more conservative to reduce the pressure of continued originations.

Floating loans are by far the least risky to originate because the borrower bears the interest rate risk. In an improving market, floating loans may reduce fallout due to price wars; however, floaters may continue to float in anticipation of continued market improvement. If the paperwork needs to be updated due to an over-hopeful borrower, should fees or penalties be assessed to cover processing costs?

In a declining market, most borrowers choose to lock in a price, but this is the time loan originators need to promote floaters to reduce market exposure. Floating loans can reduce the risk of being whipsawed in the market while trying to obtain coverage for the pipeline. Fees may be imposed up-front to lock a price quote and reduce the risk of repricing the loan if the market improves. Fees may also be required to cover loss which cannot be charged to the borrower for refinancing or special investor commitments.

Once the guarantee terms are established, policy regarding expired commitments must be determined. It is most common for loans to be repriced at the "higher of" the original quote or the then current market. In rapidly deteriorating markets, this provides additional protection from marketing losses. In improving markets, though, borrowers may walk away from their loans and begin processing with another company. Ability to negotiate price with the borrower becomes important in preventing excessive fallout due to price wars. Common sense should be used in those cases where the borrower is not responsible for the expiration.

A policy that addresses VA loans that are guaranteed when the VA changes its administered rate should be established. This policy must pay heed to VA regulations regarding rate changes, and it should be decided whether the policy will be used for FHA loans as well.

Once products and rates have been determined, the company should decide if the same pricing policies apply to all offerings. Some firms, for example, have different pricing policies for refinances or non-owner properties.

Company policy should determine if the loan must be delivered to the shipping department (or other appropriate area) within the guarantee period (or so many days after closing). The longer the time allowed for delivery, the greater the risk that the loan cannot be shipped for a specific delivery month. The company should also determine whether or not there will be a penalty for exceeding the allotted time for delivery. Some firms charge a fee equal to the price differential from one delivery month to another (this is especially true on loans delivered late from correspondents); others charge no penalty. Some companies pay incentives to processors/closers for each closed loan and disallow the incentive for loans delivered late. Branch offices may be charged for the late loans they deliver.

In order to avoid misunderstandings, pricing policies should always be in writing and made available to all appropriate personnel.

Defining Corporate Marketing Policies

It is extremely important that the board of directors define appropriate levels of authority for marketing policies. This authorization may be given to the CEO, a "marketing committee," or another such entity. It should specifically define the scope of control retained exclusively by the board and the authority given to others.

The person or entity responsible for setting prices for the products offered should be designated, as well as the replacement in case of absence. Generally, the marketing manager or the marketing committee are charged with this responsibility.

The people responsible for obtaining investor commitments should be identified as well as the guidelines. Again, this responsibility generally falls on the marketing manager or marketing committee. Parameters that could be defined include type of commitment, minimum/maximum amounts, terms of commitments, and allowable investors.

Staff should be assigned a day-to-day position manager. This person is generally the trader, and his parameters need to be specifically defined. Examples of parameters would include: setting dollar or percentage limits on long or short coverage; establishing maximum limits on the amount of unsettled commitments with any dealer (these are referred to as "dealer limits"); and specifying the risk management tools that are approved for use and the limits of each, e.g., futures, cash forwards, options on futures, or over-the-counter options.

If options are an approved tool, the trader should know the amount of his "fee budget." Often this is a percentage of annual production. Some companies limit the dollar amount of inventory that can be traded in any one day without higher levels of authority. The position manager should be responsible for marking the position to market at regularly defined intervals and notifying appropriate senior management personnel.

The person or persons with authority to establish marketing strategies should be designated. Generally, this is the CEO or marketing committee in most organizations. This group is also responsible for defining the position manager's parameters as indicated above. Examples of marketing strategies would include long/short coverage ratios; percentage of pipeline that should not be covered and the percentage to be covered with any combination of forwards, futures or options; hedge ratios; timing of the sale of inventory to maximize warehouse spreads, etc.

A written policy or procedure should be implemented that details how marketing transactions are integrated with the accounting, audit, underwriting, and shipping departments. These procedures need to include what records of each transaction should be kept and the people responsible for maintaining the records. GNMA has specific requirements regarding the marketing of GNMA securities, which they have defined as "Prudent Business Practices." These rules should be incorporated into the corporate policies and procedures.

In medium and large sized companies the position of "operations manager" can be a very effective link between the marketing and administrative departments. Some companies even have the operations manager on the marketing committee because of his or her valued input. The person holding this position is responsible for: verifying that loan product meets corporate policy and commitment guidelines and is delivered accordingly; scheduling deliveries to investors; accurate and timely funding by investors; administering pricing policies; commitment control; coordinating new investor programs and documentation requirements with underwriting, policies and procedures, and servicing departments; and relaying information on sold loans to the servicing and accounting departments, in addition to other similar duties.

The operations manager is the person who provides information on whether marketing can take advantage of an immediate price in the market and deliver $5,000,000 this afternoon. He or she is up-to-date on where departmental backlogs are occurring and where the workload is light, and attempts to juggle staffing accordingly. An effective operations manager can make the job of the marketing manager much easier while improving the flow of loans.

Institutions that use financial futures and options on futures should have a specific board-approved policy on the use of these marketing tools. Such a policy should contain, at minimum, the following elements:

- The purpose of the policy;

- Systems to be used to maintain control over the use of futures and options and the accounting requirements of these systems;

- Authorization of specific dealers;

- Authorization of specific individuals to trade these instruments;

- Authorization of daily trading limits;

- Authorization of instruments that can be used;

- Transaction control requirements for records maintenance;

- Audit control procedures;

- Internal reporting procedures;

- Authorization of entity responsible for formulating strategies that involve the use of futures or options;

- Accounting procedures to be used to record entries and maintain margin accounts; and

- Form of summary reports to be given to the Board and at what intervals.

The secret to successful marketing policies is to set a prudently appropriate level of authority and control in a comprehensive policy that requires communication of specific information to those who need to know. It is the best way to ensure that the CEO and the board of directors are always informed on the activities of the marketing department.

Organization of the Marketing Department

No structure for a marketing department can be said to be typical in this industry. Structure and reporting lines vary by company as do their relative successes. Here are some examples:

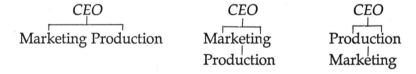

The advantage of the first structure is that the marketing and production sections can be headed by people with substantial experience in their own areas. The negative is that this structure can lead to destructive competition between the two divisions unless the CEO fosters an atmosphere of teamwork and shared goals. With the other two structures, the competitive aspect is removed, but the person reporting to the CEO must be well-experienced in both production and marketing.

Perhaps the most important consideration in structuring a marketing department is the location of the shipping division.

Most firms have this function reporting either directly to the marketing manager or to the operations manager, who in turn reports to the marketing manager. Some companies have the shipping department report to the servicing manager, with varied success.

Pricing, hedging, and trading are all functions that should report to the marketing manager.

Measuring Results

The most important tool senior management and the risk manager have available to measure results of their risk management policies is the mark-to-market report. The mark-to-market values the inventory that has been sold against the sales prices of the loans, and unsold inventory against either the current market (if the loans are not hedged) or against the value of the hedge instrument. This report details the net profit or loss position of the inventory and is the key to limiting risk. Companies that access this information on a daily basis are subject to considerably less risk than those which can only provide the information once a week. Any firm that uses futures contracts or options on futures contracts cannot prudently manage its risk without a daily mark-to-market report.

Rate environments, borrower preferences, investor requirements, and regulatory impacts all change. All of these can have a tremendous influence on mortgage banking and require a company to review its policies constantly.

Management Controls

Once comprehensive risk management policies have been developed, the key to their success is in ensuring that they are followed. Senior management must develop a mechanism whereby compliance can be verified.

This can be accomplished in several ways. One way is to authorize periodic audits by either an internal or external entity. Another is to develop automated system reports that detail exceptions to specific benchmarks.

And finally, a firm should make effective use of the traditional corporate tool—meetings. Regular meetings between the appropriate senior management personnel and the appropriate risk management personnel, where management can ask questions and keep informed on marketing activities, can be very useful. Some companies use all three techniques.

Glossary

At-The-Money: Used in dealing with options, when the strike price is equal to the market price or the underlying security.

At-The-Money Option: When the strike price is approximately equal to the market price of the underlying security.

Arbitrage: The buying and selling of mortgages, futures, contracts or mortgage-backed securities in various markets for the purpose of creating a profit from the differences in price.

Basis: Difference between the cash price of a commodity and the price of the hedge instrument in the futures market used to protect the commodity from price risk.

Basis Point: One one-hundredth of one percent. Used to describe the amount of change in yield in many debt instruments, including mortgages. Thus a bond's yield that changed from 10.50 percent to 11.25 percent would have increased 75 basis points.

Basis Risk: The chance that the basis will change, thus creating an inefficient hedge.

Bear Market: Market characterized by falling prices. A bear market in mortgage banking is caused by rising interest rates.

Bid-Ask Spread: The difference between what a dealer will bid for a security (the bid price) versus what he will offer to sell it for (the ask price).

Bull Market: Market characterized by rising prices. A bull market in mortgage banking is caused by falling interest rates.

Ca-Call: A "call on call" compound option.

Ca-Put: A "call on put" compound option.

Call Option: A contract granting the right, but not the obligation, to purchase the underlying security at a specified price (the strike price) anytime prior to or on the expiration date (see Put-Option).

Chicago Board Options Exchange (CBOE): The largest and most active standardized, organized options marketplace.

Compound Options: Basically options on options; they require that the buyer pay a fee for the right to buy an additional option at a later date, at a given strike price.

Convergence: Movement of the price of a futures contract toward the price of the underlying cash commodity. At the start of the contract, price is higher because of the time value. But as the contract nears expiration, the futures price and the cash price converge.

Cost-of-Carry: The difference between the yield on an instrument and the cost of funds to finance it.

Cross Hedge: A hedge of an asset or liability with an instrument of different characteristics.

Current Market Position: In mortgage banking, the amount of money a firm would gain or lose if it were to meet loan guarantees and mandatory commitments at today's market prices.

Delta: The unit change in the price of an option (the premium) for a unit change in the price of the underlying security.

Discount: In loan originations, a discount refers to an amount withheld from loan proceeds by a lender. In secondary market sales, a discount is the amount by which the sale price of a note is less than its face value. In both instances, the purpose of a discount is to adjust the yield upward, either in lieu of interest or in addition to interest. The rate or amount of discount depends on money market conditions, the credit of the borrower, and the rate or terms of the note.

Duration: A good estimate of the volatility or sensitivity of the market price of a bond to changes in interest rates; it measures the weighted average time until cash flow repayment.

Exercise Price: The price at which the underlying security or commodity will be delivered in the event an option is *exercised*.

Exposure: Uncovered or unhedged risk that may result in a loss. Unhedged pipeline loans create exposure to fluctuations in interest rates and other market factors.

Fallout: Percentage of pipeline expected not to close.

Financial Futures: Futures contracts based on financial instruments; the futures contract price fluctuates in relation to changes in price in the financial cash markets.

Firm Commitment: For loans, a lender's agreement to make a loan to a specific borrower under specific terms and conditions within a given time. In the secondary market or the securities market, a buyer's agreement to purchase loans (securities) under specified terms.

Floating Rate Loans: Loans that are not guaranteed an interest rate and therefore close at prevailing market rates.

Forward Discount: The difference between the cash market spot price and the forward market price.

Forward Delivery Contract: The sale of a specified quantity and type of commodity at a specified price for delivery on a specified date in the future.

Forward Sale: A contract sale between two traders for delivery of a specific asset at a fixed time in the future for a strike price to be determined today.

Free Put: A put for which no consideration or money is paid. See put option.

Fundamental Analysis: The approach to valuation that considers variables supposed to determine value (i.e., current and future earnings and risk variables) in determining the intrinsic values of individual securities.

Funding: Payment of money by lenders for a mortgage loan settlement, or receipt of money by lenders from investors that purchase mortgages.

Gamma: The unit change in the delta for a unit change in the underlying security (see delta).

Good Delivery: A term referring to all conditions of a securities delivery that must be met by the seller. These conditions include correct type of security, issuer, quantity, denomination of certificate(s), presence of any outstanding interest coupons, proper endorsement of the power of assignment, and timeliness of delivery.

Guarantees: In mortgage banking, the interest rate locks that lenders offer borrowers.

Hedge: The establishment of a position in a market that serves as a temporary substitute for the future sale or purchase of an actual commodity. The hedge position should move such that it offsets losses and/or gains in the hedger's cash position in the event of changing market conditions.

Hedge Ratio: Equates face value and yield of the cash position to that of futures contracts written. This ratio considers the effect of changing interest rates on futures and cash yields.

In-the-Money: Describes a market condition when the strike or exercise price on an option is lower than the market price, giving the option intrinsic value. (A call option is in-the-money if the strike price is below the current market price. A put option is in-the-money if the strike price is above the current market position.)

Intrinsic Value: The value of an option if it were to expire immediately. If the option's strike price is in-the-money, then it has positive intrinsic value. If the strike is out-of-the-money, then the option's intrinsic value is zero.

Liquidity: For a specific instrument, the existence of sufficient supply and demand to facilitate the establishment or termination of a position.

Long Position: The portion of a mortgage banker's inventory that has not been sold to an investor.

Long Risk Ratio: Dollar volume of mandatory plus optional commitments minus inventory loans divided by pipeline (adjusted for fallout).

Mandatory Commitment: A commitment into which loans must be delivered or penalties paid.

Mandatory Position: An agreement obligating a lender to sell or buy a particular product at a specified interest rate, price, and true date.

Margin Call: A requirement to post either capital or collateral with a broker to cover potential losses in advance on hedging positions.

Mark-to-Market Report: A report that values the inventory that has been sold against the sales price of the loans, and the unsold inventory against either current market prices or the value of the hedge instrument.

Naked Option: Selling call or put options without having a position on the underlying security. Naked options are very risky, although potentially very rewarding.

Naked Position: An uncovered or unhedged market position. For example, the position of someone who sells a call or put option without having the corresponding long or short position on the underlying security.

Net Mandatory Position: The difference, whether long or short, between the dollar volume of loans in inventory and mandatory sales.

Net Non-Mandatory Position: The difference, whether long or short, between the dollar volume of the discounted pipeline (adjusted for fallout) and optional sales.

Options Combos: Puts and calls bought and sold simultaneously in order to lock in price floors without sacrificing potential upside gains.

Options on Futures: Contracts exercised into futures contracts and traded on the Chicago Board of Trade under highly standardized terms. Contract sizes are $100,000, premiums are quoted in 64ths, and strike prices are set at two point intervals for bond futures, and at one point for T-Notes.

Option Premium: Consisting of intrinsic value and time value, the difference between the strike price and that of the underlying security.

Options Spread: The difference in premiums (prices) resulting from a combination of put and call options on the same underlying security. Strike price and expiration dates may be the same or different.

Over-The-Counter Options: Flexible O-T-C options enable the lender to purchase and sell calls as well as puts. Therefore, any side of an options transaction can be taken when structuring a hedging strategy.

Out-of-the-Money: When the strike price of the option exceeds the market price of the underlying security. The option, therefore, has no intrinsic value.

Par: The nominal, or face value, of a security.

Pair-Off: To buy out of a commitment to sell mortgages or mortgage-backed securities.

Pipeline: Loan applications in process that have not been closed at settlement.

Premium: The total price of an option contract. It consists of the sum of the intrinsic value and the time value.

Prepayment: Paying a loan before maturity. Generally, residential mortgages have a prepayment clause that allows prepayment at any time without penalty.

Price Guarantee: A price agreed upon when a futures contracts is executed.

Put Option: A contract granting the right but not the obligation to sell the underlying security at a specified price (the strike price) anytime prior to the expiration date. See call option.

Rally: A rise in prices following a sudden decline.

Regression: A statistical method of determining the change in value of a dependent variable given a change in one or more independent variables.

Relative Supply: A source of basis movement that describes the symbiotic relationship between mortgage rates and the supply of Treasuries.

Repurchase Agreement: Agreement between a buyer and a seller of securities whereby the seller agrees to buy back the securities at an agreed upon price, and usually, at a stated time.

Rolling: Buying or selling back an open position in one month and re-selling or re-buying in either a future or closer month.

Sector Spread: Describes the situation where as interest rates fall, a short Treasury hedge may need to be reduced because mortgage prices tend to rise less than those of Treasuries.

Short Position: A sale of loans or securities, including optional or mandatory forward sales as well as sales in the futures market.

Short Risk Ratio: The dollar difference between mandatory commitments and inventory loans divided by pipeline (adjusted for fallout) dollar volumes.

Split-Fee Option: A compound option that requires the buyer to pay a fee for the right to purchase an additional option at a later date and at a prearranged strike price.

Spread: (1) The markup of a price, intended to cover a seller's selling expenses and provide profit on a transaction. A spread is the difference between purchase and sale price. (2) The difference between the rate of return on assets and the rate of return on liabilities. (3) The difference between the buying and selling rate of a foreign currency. (4) The difference in prices of futures contracts of different maturities. It is a synonym for "basis." (5) To go long on one futures contract and short on another contract of a different maturity, in the hope that the spread between them will change favorably.

Standby Commitment: A commitment issued by an investor or broker dealer, in the secondary mortgage market for single-family loans, to purchase mortgages if offered. The purchaser of this commitment has the option of delivering or not delivering a specified amount of mortgages or mortgage-backed securities at a given rate within a specified time. A developer often uses a standby commitment to secure a construction loan, thereby providing time to build, lease, and qualify a project for a more favorable mandatory delivery commitment.

Stop Order: A supplemental order submitted with an initial futures trade that will be executed should the market move to or beyond the level specified. This removes the trader from his position and therefore limits his losses.

Straddle: To hold a put and call option on the same asset at the same strike price. The intent of a straddle is to profit from a large change, either up or down, in the asset's price.

Strike Price: The stated price on an options contract at which the underlying security may be bought or sold prior to or upon expiration.

Substitute Sale: Participants in the futures market do not intend to ship or receive the underlying debt instrumentns. When the firm decides to sell the mortgages, the lender purchases an identical number of futures contracts to offset the ones that were sold, thus liquidating its futures position, while simultaneously executing a mandatory forward sale. "Buying the other side."

Synthetic Call: Combining a long position with a put option. In mortgage banking, originating mortgages while simultaneously buying puts.

Synthetic Put: Combining a short position with a call option. In mortgage banking, selling mortgages forward while simultaneously buying call options.

Technical Analysis: The philosophy that past price movements indicate patterns useful for predicting future price movements for purposes of valuation.

Time Value: The value of an option above its intrinsic value.

Theta: The change in the time value of an option between points in time.

Volatility: A measure of the amount by which an instrument's price fluctuates in a given period of time.

Warehouse: Loans that are funded and awaiting sale to an investor.

Whipsaw: The quick reversal of an apparent trend in the movement of interest rates or prices. A whipsaw occurs most frequently in highly volatile markets.

Yield Curve: A chart showing the relation between interest rates on similar securities with different maturities. A graphic representation of market yield for a fixed income security plotted against the maturity of the security.

References

The following is a list of materials that have been of use in the making of this book. This bibliography, however, is by no means a complete record of all the works and sources that were consulted. It indicates the subject and range of reading upon which various risk management theories and applications are presented. In addition to the specific sources cited below, great use was made of pamphlets from selected brokerage houses, the Chicago Board of Trade, and Fannie Mae.

"The Asset Hedging Primer," *Financial Management.* Washington, D.C.: FHLMC, October, 1984.

Hedging in GNMA Mortgage Interest Rate Futures. Chicago: Chicago Board of Trade, 1975.

GNMA Mortgage Interest Rate Futures. Chicago: Chicago Board of Trade, 1975.

"Origination and Delivery of Due Bills," *GNMA Mortgage Interest Rate Futures.* Chicago: Chicago Board of Trade, 1975.

GNMA II Futures. Chicago: Chicago Board of Trade, 1984.

"Cash-Settled GNMA Proposed," Washington, D.C.: *Real Estate Finance Today*, November 8, 1985.

"Introduction to Hedging," Chicago: Chicago Board of Trade, 1984.

"Pipeline Hedging," Chicago: Chicago Board of Trade, 1985.

"Financial Instruments Markets: Cash-Futures Relationships," Chicago: Chicago Board of Trade, 1982.

"Government Securities Dealers Said to Have Big Losses from Short Squeeze in 9 1/4% Bond," Heard on the Street, *Wall Street Journal*, Dow Jones & Co. Inc. 5/23/86.

Hedging Workbook, Chicago: Chicago Board of Trade, 1984.

"Financial Futures: The Delivery Process in Brief," Chicago: Chicago Board of Trade, 1982.

"The Merrill Lynch Guide to Writing Options," Merrill Lynch, Pierce, Fenner & Smith, Inc. 2/80.

Powerhedge, Donna Reynolds, Stock Index Futures, Inc., St. Louis, 1986.

Futures and Options Strategies for Mortgage Originators, Raleigh-Reynold, St. Louis, 1984.

"An Introduction to the Interest Rate Futures Market," Chicago: Chicago Board of Trade, 1977.

"Opportunities in Interest Rates," Merrill Lynch, 1980.

"Options on Treasury Bond Futures," Chicago: Chicago Board of Trade, 1982.

"Listed Options on Debt Instruments," AMEX, Chicago Board of Trade and OCC 10/82.

"Understanding Options, a Guide to Puts and Calls," Chicago Board of Options Exchange, 1977.

"Call Option Writing Strategies," Chicago Board Options Exchange, 1975.

"Tax Consequences of Listed Put and Call Options," Thomson McKinnon, September, 1983.

"Cash—Settled GNMA Futures," Chicago: Chicago Board of Trade, 1986.

"GNMA Futures Cash Settled Contract," Chicago: Chicago Board of Trade, 1986.

"The Banker's Guide to Financial Futures," a special Conti Report, Geraldine Syzmanski, Conti Corp.

"Institutional Constant Writing Program to Enhance Portfolio Yield," Scott M. Krantz, Conti Commodity Services, Inc.

"Introduction to Financial Futures and Hedging," Neal C. Hansen, Refco, Inc.

"Cross-Hedging Fannies, Freddies and Ginnies," John W. Labuszawski, and Dennis M. Collins, *Mortgage Banking*, June, 1986.

"Secondary Mortgage Market," Michelle Campbell, *Mortgage Banking*, 1986.

"Hedging, Balancing Risk & Reward," Gary L. Perlin and Jane Piemonte, *Mortgage Banking*, May, 1986.

"Secondary Mortgage Markets," Richard Hamecs, *Mortgage Banking*, March, 1986.

"Calculating a Risk Profile for the Mortgage Pipeline," Paul E. Tuttle, Jr., *Mortgage Banking*, March, 1986.

"Increased Leverage and Decreased Risk," Richard M. Kaplan, Douglas R. Hiscano, David Weiner and Ernst J. Mikosch, *Mortgage Banking*, March, 1986.

"Analyzing Competing Pools," Susan D. Mara, *Mortgage Banking*, March, 1986.

"Guaranteed Delivery," Les Parker, *Mortgage Banking*, March, 1986.

"Strategic Pipeline Hedging," Sirri Ayayetin and Stephen R. Rigsbee, *Mortgage Banking*, March, 1986.

"What's New at the Board of Trade," Thom Thompson, *Mortgage Banking*, March, 1986.

"Intricate Workings of Risk Management," Michael R. Wise, Mortgage Banking, February, 1986.

"Secondary Mortgage Markets," Richard M. Hamecs, *Mortgage Banking*, February, 1986.

"Understanding Options on Futures," Jeanne Cairns Sinquefield, *Mortgage Banking*, July, 1982.

"Improving Yields with Arbitrage Trading," Ted Thomas, *Mortgage Banking*, July, 1982.

"FNMA'S CMBS Program: Access to the Capital Market," J. Donald Clink, *Mortgage Banking*, May 1982.

"Pricing Mortgage-Backed Securities in the Forward Market," Susan D. Mara, *Mortgage Banking*, November, 1985.

"Secondary Mortgage Markets," Kerrie Kyde, *Mortgage Banking*, November, 1985.

"Options: GNMA vs. Bond Futures," Laurie S. Goodman, *Mortgage Banking*, September, 1986.

"Proliferation of Mortgage-Backed Securities," Joseph Hu, *Mortgage Banking*, September, 1985.

"Private Conduits Carve a Niche in the Market," Deborah Whiteside, *Mortgage Banking*, September, 1985.

"Adding Variety to the Product Mix," Jess Lederman, *Mortgage Banking*, October, 1985.

"New Opportunities: Risks in the Secondary Market," Charles E. Reed, *Mortgage Banking*, Special Issue—1984.

"Controlling Mortgage Pipeline Risk," John W. Labuszewski & James F. Meisner, *Mortgage Banking*, Special Issue—1984.

"CMO's and How They Grow," Richard M. Hamecs, *Mortgage Banking*, Special Issue—1984.

"Structured Financing; Making a Defference," Michael J. BeVier & John W. Biasucci, *Mortgage Banking*, Special Issue—1984 and July, 1984.

"Something Old, Something New: GNMA II Program Revisited," Susan D. Mara, *Mortgage Banking*, July, 1985.

"You Have to Know When to Hold Them and When to Fold Them," Richard Kaplan, Peter Corey and Val Schurowliew, *Mortgage Banking*, July, 1985.

"Secondary Marketing Strategies," Parts I & II, Jess Lederman, *Mortgage Banking*, May-June, 1985.

"Hands-On Risk Management," Felix Beck, *Mortgage Banking*, May, 1985.

"Special Deals for Special Needs," William T. Madden, *Mortgage Banking*, May, 1985.

"Expanding the MBS Investor Base," Rebecca Boyd, *Mortgage Banking*, May, 1985.

"Hedging Risk: Forward Market or Futures Market," Robert S. Smith and James J. Lennox, *Mortgage Banking*, September, 1984.

"Option Spread Strategies for Protection," David L. Kaplan, *Mortgage Banking*, November, 1984.

"Pricing Discount ARM's in the Secondary Market," Jess Lederman, *Mortgage Banking*, August, 1984.

"Wholesale Mortgage Banking: Growth Industry," Michael Stamper and Susan Sheppard-Haun, *Mortgage Banking*, August, 1984.

"CMO'S Transform Credit Markets," Dr. Victor Cholewicki, *Mortgage Banking*, February, 1985.

"Measuring the Maturity of a Mortgage Security," Scott M. Pinkus and Susan D. Mara, *Mortgage Banking*, February, 1985.

"MIDANET: Strategic Planning Against the Paper War," Michael F. Coffey, *Mortgage Banking*, April, 1985.

"Options Letter," Morgan Stanley, January, 1986.

"Cash-Settled GNMA Futures Will Track Current Mortgage Production," Thomas G. Thompson, Financial Exchange (Chicago Board of Trade), January-February, 1986.

"Choose the Right Fuel for Your CMO Vehicle," Rebecca T. Boyd, *Bottomline*, November, 1985.

"Characteristics and Risks of Standardized Options," Thomson McKinnon, September, 1985.

"Hedging Alternatives for Mortgage Originators: A Risk Management Analysis," Mortgage Finance Research, Shearson Lehman Mortgage Securities, February, 1985.

Mortgage Banking Basics, John W. Heamon, Washington D.C.: Mortgage Bankers Association, 1984.

Real Estate Finance and Housing: 1986 Outlook and Fact Book, Mortgage Bankers Association, 1986.

Marketing Information and Position Reports, Ronald Rowland, Mortgage Bankers Association, 1985.

"Rocket Scientists Are Revolutionizing Wall Street," *Business Week*, April 21, 1986.

"Ginnie Maes Are Attractive at Current Rates Despite Loan Prepayments, Some Analysts Say," Heard on the Street, *The Wall Street Journal*, March 13, 1986.

"Prepays Bring Arbitrage Opportunities," *National Thrift News*, April 28, 1986.

Index

A

adjustable rate mortgages (ARMs), 7
allocated report, 40, 43 45
arbitrage, 17, 78
at-the-money, 92, 102

B

bar chart formations, 67
basic risk, 10 11, 16, 20, 22, 24, 97
Black Scholes, 30

C

call option, 25
calls, 25
calls on calls, 35
calls on puts, 35
cash forward sales, 14
Chicago Board of Trade, 17, 33